WEEDING YOUR GARDEN

CHANGE AND PURIFICATION

Saint Germain

with

Lah Rahn Ananda
Aka Gordon Corwin II

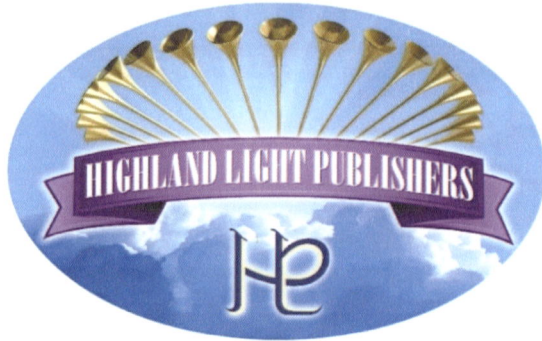

WEEDING YOUR GARDEN

CHANGE AND PURIFICATION

෨෬

Sanit Germain

Portrait Marius Fine Art

Books by This Author

❧❧

THE SAINT GERMAIN CHRONICLES COLLECTION
A Journey Into Practical Spirituality

VICTORY FOR THE SOUL
Relationships That Work

RISING ABOVE
A Journey To Higher Dimensions

TRUE COMPASSION
Merging Love Into Oneness

TRUST AND BETRAYAL

DUALITY
In Perspective

MANIFESTATION MAGIC
Saint Germain

GORDON CORWIN II aka LAH RAHN ANANDA   Amazon   www.SaintGermainbooks.com

CONTENTS

PICTURE DIAGRAMS
AND
DRAWINGS

Over the past twenty-five years, Saint Germain has transmitted to me, as an Earth Partner of the Ascended Realm and as the channel of His Celestial Purple Masterful Wisdom book series, ... in excess of 50 concise visual images depicting Spiritual energies. For your clarity and enlightenment, fifteen of these picture diagram / drawings have been carefully selected to be included for you in WEEDING YOUR GARDEN, CHANGE AND PURIFICATION. *Enjoy them, My Friends.*

Love, Lah Rahn

TRANSCENDING INTO UNCONDITIONAL LOVE LIGHT

BODY - SPECTRUM OF LIFE

HIGHER DIMENSIONAL ONENESS EXPERIENCING

ONENESS (2)

SELF-TALK REBIRTHING

OBSERVATION DYNAMICS

CONSCIOUS PERCEPTIONS

EMBRACING DUALITY

HEALING JUDGMENTS INTO ONENESS HARMONY

THE TRUTH

GRAND PURIFICATION PROCESS

JOY OF BEING PRESENT

THE SPARK OF BEING HUMAN

BOOK COVER GRAPHIC
THE LOTUS FLOWER

This elegant lotus flower artwork has been especially chosen by Saint Germain as the unique image to cover this book, to symbolize purity, enlightenment, and rebirth of Human consciousness.

The ethereal beauty of the lotus flower is a symbol of enlightenment, typically evoking feelings of Spiritual awakening, harmony, peace, tranquility, and The Divine. It represents transformation, rising from ignorance to Wisdom, from darkness to light, basking its open petals in the sunlight.

For this book, the exquisite Lotus Flower bloom artwork energy holds depth and symbolism surrounding Humanity's current, imminent, and existential choice for transformation from Ego-separation into Oneness, "a fateful awakening that urgently hangs in the balance for this Human civilization's survival", Saint Germain.

The many colors of the Lotus Flower you see on this cover majestically combine whites, saffrons, pinks, yellows, reds, blues, greens and purples, ... as symbolism of various stages of Spiritual awakening, embracing Purity, Compassion, Love, Devotion, Wisdom, Mysticism, and Divine Enlightenment.

Enjoy with many Blessings, Lah Rahn.

OVERVIEW

he Age of Aquarius is ushering All Earthly Beings into a pivotal time of existential choice. The future of this current Human *civilization* hangs in the balance ... of either changing to adopt a bright new consciousness of *Truth* leading to Oneness, <u>or</u> to continue its habitual toxic downward path of Ego-dominated separation and lethal conflict, leading to a foretold fate of a technology crazed self-destruction. Your *individual choice for change* at this point will have profound impact upon the remainder of your current Earthly lifetime, as well as marking a magnificent milestone of your Soul healing.

As Saint Germain, I lovingly bring to you this urgently needed healing and *compelling solution for change in consciousness*, ... an *individual* purification *choice* of massive consequential importance. I speak of the imperative, time-critical change to alter Humanity's present course of self-destruction for this civilization ... with devastating reversion back to the stone age.

WEEDING YOUR GARDEN presents an advanced, and achievable, fully encompassing cleansing process to change and heal individual thinking patterns from Judgment-making to Observation-making, ... bridged by honoring the Truth. Standing squarely before you is a momentous time of personal *choice for change leading to Unity and Oneness*.

Be aware that along with your World's recent massive advance-ments in technology, ... and an *unshakeable obsession for more and more*, ... comes an extensional and crowning need for a <u>corresponding advancement in Human consciousness</u> ... a requisite upward vibrational shift ... a need blatantly ignored by the masses of Humanity. Rising Above from the depths of your current Third Dimensional behaviors of Ego-separation, wars, and destruction will be required to now avoid collapse of Humanity's current World civilization, some 5000 – 6000 plus years of historical Earth time. <u>This book sources a pathway to an upward shift of consciousness,</u> CHANGE AND PURIFICATION, <u>to balance energies that are tipping the scale to allow destructive technologi-cal implementations to prevail.</u>

1

This book guides dedicated Ones to transform old habitual and toxic Human thinking patterns of *Judgment-making in Ego separation* <u>into</u> a p*urified modality of Observation-making of 'What is' within the Domain of Truth* ... a common denominator between Humans leading to Oneness beyond Third Dimensional separation behaviors and beliefs.

To prepare you for this momentous change, this win-win transformation process leads you through optional *external* preparations as well as *required internal* preparations for heightened abilities to manage Self-love, Self-talk, Self-discipline, Self-Observation, A quiet mind, Chakra cleansing, Resistance to Change, and more, ... empowering you to now begin this life-changing upward ascent toward *individual Freedom and a Oneness* once known to some of you in Atlantis!

Rewards for Mastery of this purification process transport willing and dedicated Ones away from the Ego-separation trap <u>into</u> the *'What is' of Truth*, blending Earth World collective consciousness into harmony, ... while <u>also</u> *reserving inside your own personal Universe* a full lifetime of unbounded individual Human experiences, thoughts, feelings, sensations, and emotions to be consciously observed.

Allow yourself to finally take this life-changing forward leap *of* Weeding <u>your</u> Garden with *Change and Purification* ... to make this delightful and profound transformation yours forever,
My Dearest Ones.

In your service with Blessings and Love,

Saint Germain

Through Lah Rahn Ananda

ere We are, once again. We Above are observing, along with You, the evolutionary process of HUMAN life on planet Earth, where current events give rise to tasty morsels of Wisdom for the taking …Wisdom that can be recognized, and viscerally ingested, and wisely incorporated into an evolving consciousness … all nestled in the full HUMAN EXPERIENCE of Being awake and present while living in the Earth School.

Weeding your Garden, Change and Purification, can literally be viewed as an emotional cleansing process. Here together, We are focusing on upon healing *the way you process* your feelings, emotions, and reactions to circumstances and issues that surface, omni-present in a Human livestream. For All Humanity, *weeding out and transmuting emotional reactions that result in judgments* is now essential along the path of higher evolvement. A failure to Master this process unfortunately holds Ones individually captive in Ego-judgment patterns … a lower vibration that has sadly entrapped and ensnared Humans in a separated 3rd Dimension of consciousness … for eons upon end ... unaware of the Wisdom herein to elevate themselves into Truth leading to Oneness.

Tempting it is … to experience a thought, feeling or emotion, only to allow this to collapse into an automatic Ego-judgment reaction pattern as a <u>*habit.*</u>

Notice how this behavior has its way with <u>you?</u>

Transmuting this behavior is the subject for today.

Weeding Your Garden is offered here as a powerful advanced healing process along your life path of Evolvement. In this transmission, as Saint Germain, I shall highlight one of the most abundant, fast growing, and pesky weeds that pop up in Human gardens of life …. *in your garden.* That would be the habitual judgment-making behavior.

The first part of this work is where I groom your consciousness *before y*ou are placed at the base camp of Mt. Everest to begin this healing ascent to the very top. The top marks the apex point at which you have replaced habitual Ego-judgment making with automatic Observations honoring and focusing upon the 'What is' of Truth.

Re-wiring

Together, We are re-programming your thinking patterns that hold you captive in Ego- separation, away from Oneness, ... because of an old, often traditional, judgment-making habit, yes? Purification is waiting ... for you to <u>extract these weeds, to clean up your Garden,</u> and <u>to prevent further weed poppings-up, ... for the remainder of this natural lifetime!</u>

Mounting the task of re-wiring a major part of One's Human consciousness into such closer Divine Alignment will require advanced preparation on your part to equip you for this journey. To follow, I enlarge upon *external and internal* resources, to tune up your core abilities for mounting the transformation ahead ... *and actually making the ascent!*

I reiterate for your clarity, ... <u>Weeding Your Garden presents an advanced, fully encompassing cleansing process to change and heal individual thinking patterns from Judgment-making to Observation-making, ... honoring the Truth and its *bridge* to Oneness.</u>

Standing before you is a momentous and existential time of personal choice, Dear Friends.

To accomplish this seemingly super-Human consciousness *Change and Purification feat* ... that has defied this civilization for thousands of Earth years ... a Divining One needs *Be prepared for this Change*!

 To follow, I include advanced preparation essentials, spoken as *essential* resources, for your success in transforming these old habitual and toxic Human thinking patterns <u>into</u> a p*urified modality of Observation-making of the 'What is' within the Domains of Truth and Oneness. Once inset in place, these two Domains become <u>common denominators</u> within Human thinking patterns.* When Humans then share 'the Truth' as a common guideline and point of reference, a beautiful harmony of confluent collective consciousness is born. Can you see this?

 I will lead you through *external preparation options* as well as *required internal* preparations to heighten and tune up your abilities ... as I have earlier spoken, addressing Self-love, Embracing change, A quiet mind, Changeable, Overcoming resistance to Change, Self-talk, Self-discipline, Self-Observation, Chakra cleansing, and more, Full Spectrum Life, and Human Light Body ... to now equip you to begin this life-changing upward ascent toward individual Freedom and a Oneness once known to some of you in Atlantis!

At the outset, My Dear Lads and Lassies, let Us add a bit of levity to our Grand sojourn.
Below I have constructed a picture / diagram to call forth your current understanding or knowing about key puzzle pieces dancing together in the Human Condition. Try your hand at filling in the blanks!

13

Saint Germain

Through Lah Rahn Ananda

Experiencing Oneness

The Grand Prize

Test Your Spiritual IQ by Naming the 4 Circles

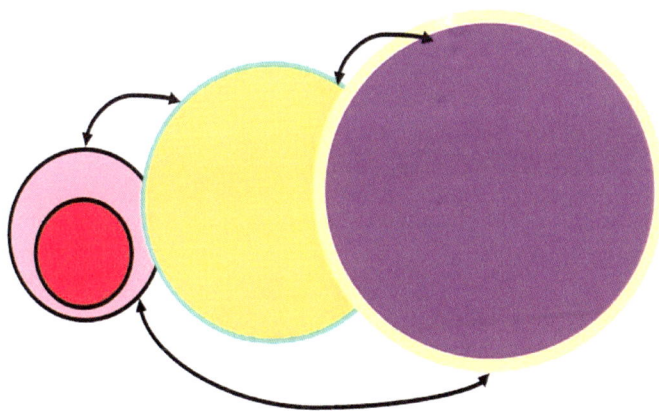

Honoring Self-love

In these times where the need for *constructive Change* is paramount, I encourage you to call forth your surrendered Higher-self to serve you with Self-love ... in addition to calling forth Blessings from the Realm of Ascended Spirit to support you in this charge.

Cultivate patience and self-care, Dear Ones, as embarking on this process will require all the wherewithal that you can muster!

Purging a life-long habit of judgment-making is admittedly a formidable task of change , indeed, for *any* Human.

A famous historical philosopher of your current Earth civilization cycle, Plato of Greece, related that a toxin in the body can be more easily purged and cleansed away with a physic, while toxins of the mind be <u>extremely difficult and time consuming to purge and eliminate, ... if at all!</u>

And so it is, We shall, nonetheless, start today in *optimism* with Self-love and cleansing. ... with you as a relationship partner with yourself!

Self-Care
in these times of Change

 Lovingly Caring for Oneself throughout this
Cleansing and Purification **process of** WEEDING Y♡UR
GARDEN, … **is of the highest importance for you.
I will hold your heart and be available to you
when you call. You must do your part also!**
 The 'Choice for Change' **you are invited to
tackle here, … by your Soul and by Ourselves
Ascended, … is massive in scope. You shall
discover its impact as you proceed.**

 In response to enormous Change, **the Human
mind and body will predictably react in ways
that need your Self-loving care and tendering.
Many are feeling tired. This is to be expected. In
time, it shall pass.**
 Nonetheless, this condition clearly underscores
your need **to follow a loving and disciplined self-
care routine, …** *to forward your own Well-being*,
My Dearest Ones.

 Feeling tired is a common condition *for those
Awakening, and/or for Ones undergoing specific
transformational change by a process*, **such as
Weeding Your Garden. Intensified body
sensations, thoughts, feelings, and emotions
during transformation come with the territory,
Folks!**

What about the specifics of Self-care? We urge you to give particular attention to:

Drinking extra amounts of purified fresh water,

Getting generous amounts of sleep,

Allowing yourself adequate times to rest,

Eating a healthy diet w/ greens/ antioxidants and fiber,

Tendering your <u>Self-talk</u> with Love.

Regular exercise, on a daily basis,

Meditating daily, morning and before supper,

Sweeping yourself repeatedly with the Violet Flame.

And

Being patient with

yourself.

You yourself are charged with filling in the blanks for your *individual situation and needs.*

Be Self-love.

SELF-LOVE

Your Inter-personal Relationship

"If you would be loved, love, and be loveable."
— Benjamin Franklin

As We embrace the many parts of Relationship dynamics, a fundamental starting point and a wonderful building block to stand upon is
your own Self-love.

Here is a *basis of You* as a relationship partner, and a grand part
of *your own inter-personal structure of consciousness, that you
yourself bring to the party,*
from day one!

Saint Germain

.

This relationship with yourself, embracing your Self-love dynamic, is so key when tackling   a task of

this magnitude, as you shall soon see. Be kind and allow yourself to adjust and re-balance along this journey. The *way you process* thoughts, feelings, emotions, observations, <u>and</u> judgments … <u>is about to be re-wired</u>. Letting go of certain attachments may surface for you on the way, among other issues.

   Yes, I admit, purifying a *life-long habi*t can be most challenging … and you deserve to have the finest Love and care along this road.

   If you choose to *<u>follow through</u>* with My invitation *to* *Weed your Garden with Change and Purification*, … you will be soon aware of these many *interlocking process elements* to follow.

Permission and Self-love

Giving One's Self *permission to allow change*
becomes an opening move ... a fundamental
choice of Self-love!
Let your intuition and inner knowing be your
guide as you consciously sort out your personal
choices for change.

Yes, there will be *consequences* that inevitably
raise their heads along your journey.
Synchronicities, irony, surprises, joys, newly
discovered Freedom, and startling life lessons
are all in the mix!

Embracing Change

Here and now, it is high time WE join together the energies of Spirit and Humanity upon Earth ... in a newly brilliant partnership.

This conjunction opens harmonic blending of a Spirit-plane energy quotient regarding change for the common good ... with *Human potential for enlightenment as the bonus.*

The focus of such Change is *wisely* lain upon mutable behaviors of Mankind. As We proceed, let Us distinguish between those things which can be changed by Free-will, with those things *not* thusly changeable.

Our conservation about energy would focus Us upon selecting the changeables, for starters Folks.

An old adage reminder:

'Bless me Oh Lord to *wisely* attempt changing things I *can* change, recognize things which I *cannot* change, and the Wisdom to know the *difference* between the two'.

While approaching this mammoth *Change and Purification* process at hand, appreciate that you have the Free-will choice to harness the
Power of Change.

And further, the choice
to apply this energy to *harmonize Changeables into Divine Alignment, hopefully with ease and Grace.*

The Phenomenon

Change itself poses multiple challenges for All Humanity, and herein now for you individually.

Among the Kingdoms upon Earth, ... Human, plant, animal, bacterial, etc., there is a common reaction to change, which threatens to throw a desired balance off-kilter, ... a change from *comfort* that the Status Quo can offer ... in the 3rd Dimension, I must add. (Master chuckles haaa hmmm).

A new rock in the fish tank will send fish into a tizzy, have you noticed?

Unfamiliar energies, ... new and strange, ... different circumstances ... may require new Human behaviors, ... situations that involve adopting new habit patterns, releasing old habits, abandoning attachments, reforming

new and accurate recollections of experiences,
... releasing the Status Quo, …
deviating from 'standard tradition', etc. etc.,
… **All can be disorienting and upsetting to Humans,** *collectively and individually.*

  Individually, the onset of change may cause
        confusion,
        stress,
        rapid heartbeat,
        increased body temperature,
        rapid eye movement,
        sleeplessness,
        anxiety,
        fear,
        survival concerns,
        anger,
        pleasant excitement,
        anticipation,
        anxiety,
        dissatisfaction,
        worry,
        and for more enlightened individuals,
        joy,
        happiness,
        pleasant emotions,
        peace,
        neutral reaction,
        no reaction whatsoever,
          and more.

Beware, however, that *this particular Change* *on your table* is more than altering a simple toxic opinion or a shallow belief, … but a courageous undertaking to change a deeply imbedded life-long
THINKING PATTERN!

Can you see where I am going … to summon your highest and finest dedication to make this change and bring your Highest-self into Divine Alignment?

Your process of changing an old, automatic habit of judgment-making can trigger *your own special set of individual* emotions, reactions, thoughts and feelings … that will require awareness, attention, modulation, and management, … and use of all of your *preparations* for this process, … as you move through *Purification and Change*!

Ignoring My guidance at this point could block you progress right here and now. If so, you can look forward to remaining stuck playing in your own little 3rd Dimensional sandbox of Ego-dominated judgments and separation from Oneness, both Human and Cosmic.

Overcoming Ego-resistance
to Change

Prime yourself to be alert _for this upcoming 'changeable change', a_ purifying pattern shift of consciousness that your Soul is awaiting!

  In general of course, be aware of your *inborn, sometimes cellular resistance to change as a Human*, … though perhaps lessened by your possible current state of evolvement. Remember, this level of Human change is Extraordinary, and seen by some to be super-human. Does your Atlantean Soul memory have recollection? (Master chuckles hhha   hmmm) **Alright!**

  We address here a specific change, … a CHANGE that brings a Human thought pattern into _a new refined energy of simply embracing the reality of 'what is, without_

embellishment.

> At the point when your Ego-consciousness lets go of resistance … and decides to release its attachment to BURDENSOME Judgment-making, … and all of its entwining tentacles of separation, … you shall be on your way to experiencing a breakthrough to a new Freedom.
>
> **Trust Me!**

No longer burdened by this pesky beast of judgment, a flood of Freedom becomes a refreshing upward turning point in the quality of your life.

Thusly, Ones unburdened from polarized separation. … happily relate to Us Above, with a sigh of relief, … their Gratefulness, Happiness and Joy surrounding this realization that noticeable change is rewarding their dedication and discipline, now gaining traction.

When this realization occurs, a brilliant new Horizon of life will be yours. Trust Me, My Dear Ones!

And to be clear, until you make this choice to shift and this becomes your reality, … to actually change to a new habit, … you are opting to continue carrying the 'beast of judgment burden', … upon your shoulders *as one part of your Human suffering ... in contrast to moving beyond resistance and choosing Self-love.*

TRANSCENDING INTO UNCONDITIONAL LOVE

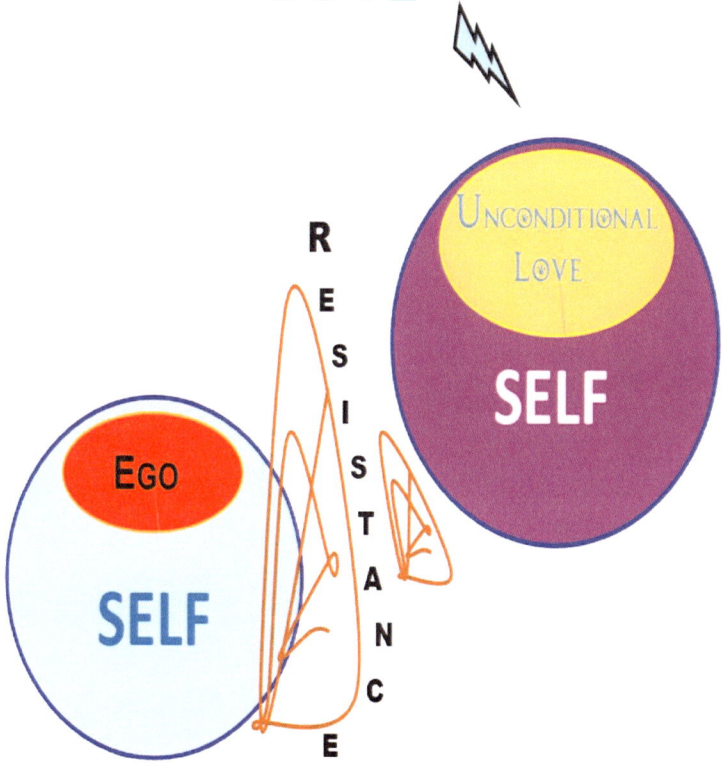

R
E
S
I
S
T
A
N
C
E

UNCONDITIONAL
LOVE

SELF

EGO

SELF

A Quiet Mind

By this point along your Spiritual path, you have no doubt encountered meritorious disciplines designed to calm, modulate, balance, and develop a harmonious mind-body conjunction.

Among these are Yoga, Meditation, Sound healing, Incense, Aroma therapy, Candle Light, Fresh flowers, Crystals, Incense, Reiki, certain Music, deep Sleep, proper Rest and more. Choose as you will.

Today, as We engage in this healing transformational process, I urge you, as Saint Germain, *to establish and maintain a regular daily practice of Transcendental Meditation.* Give yourself 20 minutes, early morning and again before your dinner, … a time period to float into a *detached thoughtless state*, … into a personal sanctuary of calm and relaxation, … fully departed and detached from the rigors of your daily Human life.

With a calm mind, your consciousness will be more accepting of the Wisdom I offer.

Bless yourself with Transcendental Meditation Folks, with this delightful, mindless mini-vacation, in a safe, private, quiet space, … wherever that may be.

<u>Sorting Out Your Changeables</u>

Identifying those things within your own personal universe that *you consciously deem as Changeable* ... is paramount for clarity.

The prime changeable at the top of today's Spirit list is: Changing the habitual behavior of <u>Judgment-making</u> into a new behavior habit of <u>Observation -making</u> !

One such truly *chooseable* choice is to make this change <u>now</u>, ... in full awareness.

And yes, some circumstances in life present no choices for change, and could be called 'unchangeables'... examples would include being at the effect of Karma, Duality, Solar cycles, the Truth, Divine Law, Universal Law, etc.

Can you see how <u>responsibility</u> for wisely using *your Free-will choice* is involved here when choosing to make a Judgment <u>or</u> <mark>choosing a neutral, non-polarized Observation?</mark>

Also, on top of this, if Judgments <u>be</u> your continued choice, be aware such choices harbor *Self-illusion that can befall* as part of the Human condition. Oh Dear, the plot thickens! (Master chuckles haaa hhaaaa).

> An Ego consciousness will often trick you <u>into a choice of illusion</u>, where choosing judgment vs. a neutral observation will appear more enticing, to make you feel better, feel right, feel dominant, important, powerful, wise, etc. etc.

<mark>As part of such illusion, the <u>absence</u> of TRUTH bears a high cost: You are trapped, out of alignment! You are saddled with the burden of judgment-making. And in this respect, *you have forfeited your Freedom.*</mark>

Figuratively, such burden is oft observed from Above as a choice to '<u>continue</u> carrying the 'ball and chain of Human suffering' trapped in the separation of the Third Dimension of consciousness,

a sad condition rampant in your World.

Multiply tens of thousands upon thousands (squared) of your judgments piled on top of each other, held in your belief system, ... and where are you now? How would you describe *Your own* state of consciousness Or Oneness?

_____

_____

_____

_____

_____

_____

_____

_____

_____

_____

_____

Few Humans realize the heavy burden of *maintaining judgments 'in place' by continuously re-justifying and strengthening and then reenforcing these judgments*, ... so their Egos can continue to BE RIGHT and Dominate The True Higher Self!
A high price to pay, indeed!

Do you see possibilities for brilliant rays of Enlightenment and Oneness to appear along this path according to the choices You make?

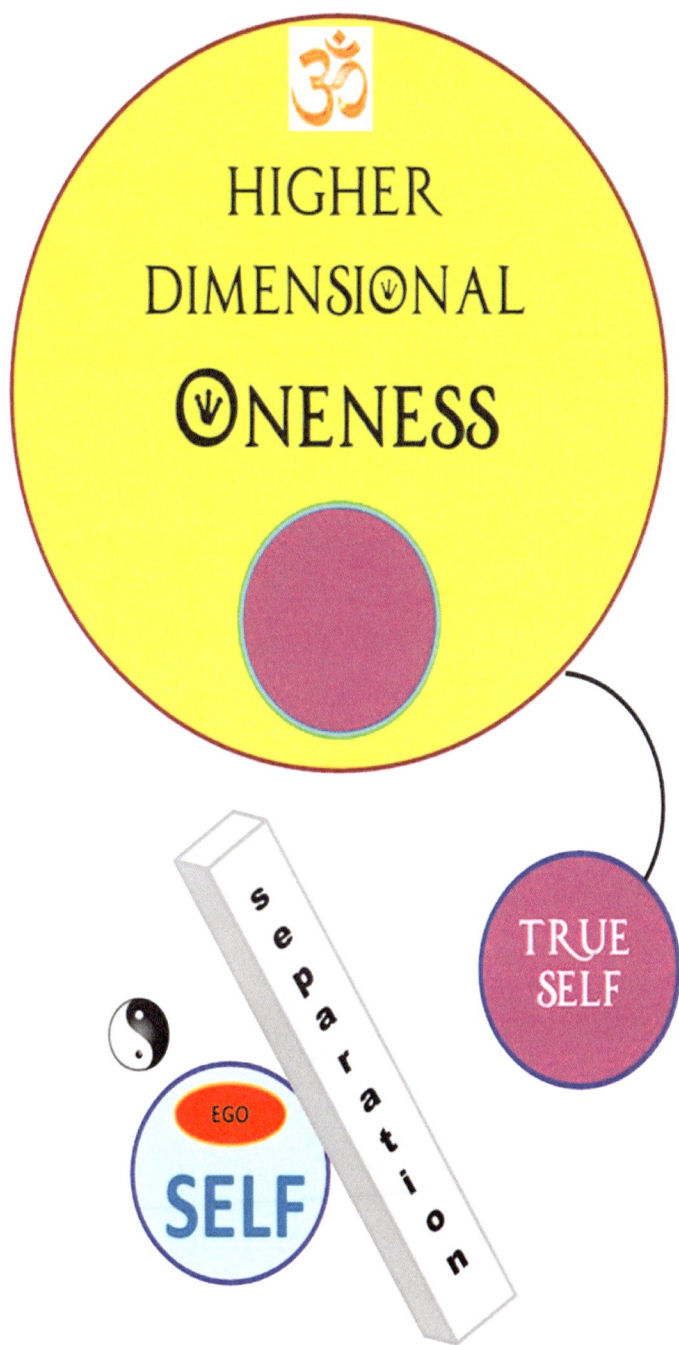

HIGHER

DIMENSIONAL

ONENESS

separation

EGO

SELF

TRUE
SELF

Does this possibility for change motivate you to engage in Weeding Your Garden, **ultimately choosing alignment with Truth, Your True Self, and ONENESS?**

∽✿∽

Full Spectrum of Life

Observation and Awareness of your <u>Full Spectrum of Life Experiences,</u> <u>…</u> including your <u>thoughts, emotions and feelings, … just as these come to you, …</u> all become integral ingredients in the process of healing the habit of judgment-making.

Embracing your Full Horizon of life experiences is essential. We could say this spectrum is *the very subject matter of Life that you are so unceasingly tempted to Judge!*

Indeed, these *life experience ingredients* do offer tempting food that would feed a hungry Ego- consciousness lurking in the shadows.

My following color diagram shows a meaningful perspective meant to illustrate *an elevating Earthly Path of full Life Experiences*, … with transforming feelings, emotions, thoughts, and life lessons included … transmuted and Rising to a *Human Light Body consciousness*.

Within the Earth School curriculum, an incarnated Human Being may at some elevated point occupy this Light Body fully standing upon Earth … *before* transition ... in an advanced state of enlightenment. The following Light Body picture / diagram illustrates the beauty of this placement in the full spectrum of Human Life.

I shall leave *succeeding Soul path options, however,* for discourse upon another day, My Good Curious Ones. Such an indulgence at this point may stretch the limits of your current pay grade. (Master chuckles, hhhmmmm hmmmm).

The Earth School's Ladder of Spiritual Ascension has many sufficiently challenging rungs to keep you on course for now, … you may have noticed? Let this progression of escalating *Full Life Experiences* bless you with Life path perspectives, … leading into this Brilliant Violet Flame Light Body transformation while incarnated in your Human skin.

᪥᪥

LIGHT BODY

LOVE
JOY
ONENESS
EUPHORIA
PEACE
HAPPINESS

A FULL Human Life Experience
PERCEPTIONS
SENSATIONS
FEELINGS
THOUGHTS
EMOTIONS

HUMAN BEING

Drinking from

The Cup of Youth

Preparations For Weeding

Mounting the task of re-wiring a major part of One's Human consciousness into closer Divine Alignment will require *external* and *internal* preparation on your part.

To follow, I mention *internal* resources, as tuning up your Self-love, Self-talk, Meditation, Balancing Chakras, and Self-discipline at a minimum. These are endogenous healings that take root deeply within you, within your consciousness extending into your full body.

Additional *external resources* are also available, as earlier mentioned options. These exogenous props work to some extent upon the energy field of you. Be clear that <u>physical external objects purchased in a Spiritual store or upon your Amazon will *not* escalate or propel you into Divine Alignment Folks</u>! If it were only that easy!

That said, there *are* valuable physical objects that can assist in their own way. These serve to open up your consciousness to make ready for *Weedng Your Garden.*

Examples of physical objects and sound vibrations may include: the Human voice, flute, chimes, Tibetan bowls, crystals, crystal bowls, Masterful likeness portraits, stringed instruments, and more.
   When played in harmonic tones that vibrate in tune with the Universe and your Soul-self, emanated sounds can soften and open your chakra energy centers.
   Also, aroma therapy, sage, and beautiful flowers serve nicely to attune you. I recommend that you avail yourself of whichever of these resources resonate with you … and rock your boat! (Master chuckles Hmmm Hmmm mm).

AND …Make no mistake, such *exogenous* resources, as I mention, … are clearly NO substitute for *internal* healings.

Spiritual dabblers often bask in complacent illusion and confusion between *internal and the external resources.*

๛๛

Alright! I've kept you in suspense long enough, Folks. Here are the answers. (Master chuckles haaa hmmm)

Saint Germain

Through Lah Rahn Ananda

Experiencing Oneness

The Grand Prize

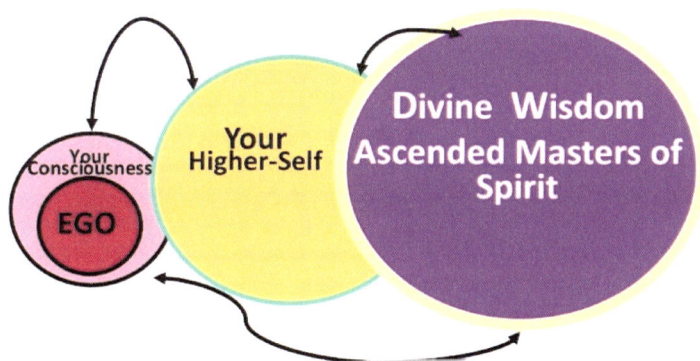

Your Consciousness

EGO

Your Higher-Self

Divine Wisdom
Ascended Masters of Spirit

Self-talk

This re-training to Weed Your Garden will also need a well-managed discipline of your Self-talk. As a prerequisite to this advanced weeding process, Ones are advised to have their <u>Self-talk management skills well honed, and instilled at the outset</u>. The following diagram illustrates the importance of *purified Self-talk*, leading you into 5th Dimensional territory and beyond. Ego-sourced judgment-making falls into the lower 3rd Dimensional segment, a space that We Above intend you to vacate and rise Above!

Choosing to shift Judgments into Observations is a giant leap upward for your consciousness, Folks. You will notice this as you proceed, … if you follow My instructions.

   As for your Ego, … acknowledge its importance in stepping aside while you viscerally meld this challenging healing into your present consciousness. Thank your Ego in advance for stepping aside to allow your heightened evolvement to proceed!

   Imagine that you are standing naked in the base camp at the foot of Mt. Everest … awaiting the starting signal from your guide, Yours truly, … to signal beginning the long ascent that awaits ahead.

Self-Talk Rebirthing

A LIFE CHANGING PROCESS WHERE
INTERNAL CONVERSATIONS MERGE WITH
HIGHEST- SELF THOUGHTS

Lower Dimensional Sourcing

Belief System

EGO

Opinions

EGO

SELF-TALK

SELF-SURRENDER

5th Dimensional Sourcing

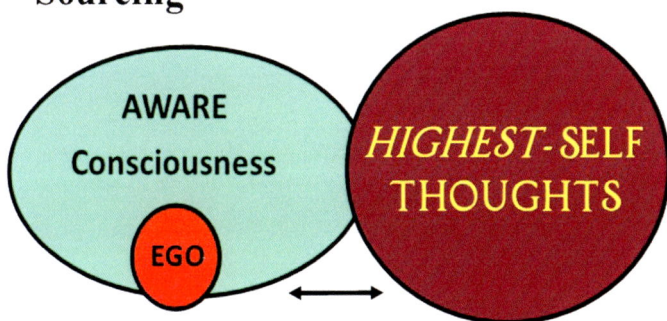

AWARE Consciousness

EGO

*HIGHEST-*SELF THOUGHTS

OPENING YOUR PATH INTO

UNITY AND ONENESS

Cleansing and Rebalancing Your Chakras

During the re-wiring preparation, in addition to giving attention and focus upon your Self-love, … rebalancing your Chakras will also be needed to hold you open to this humongous change at hand ... Y*our change* of thinking patterns.

Especially important in the 3rd and 5th Dimensions, the Chakras can be balanced, cleansed, and healed with daily regularity, through enlightened practices of the Tao combined with Ascended Realm touches delivered with Lord El Morya's Blessings. This cleansing process shows up at these Dimensional levels for the fortunate, *males and females alike, … you men may be delighted to know.* (Master chuckles haaa hhmmm)

In a sense, this is a *vibrational decontamination rinse, among other things. It is* orchestrated from Above, accessible for ongoing daily and/or nightly <u>Chakra energy center balancing</u> … healing, purification and realignment, … gratis.

During this process, energies move up and down the spine, pulsating along the spinal column, emanating from the *root chakra* area and pelvic region, rising up along the spine to the brain.

At times, energy sensations last for several minutes duration, and keep repeating in cycles, similar to sets of breaking ocean waves licking the sands of your beaches, in a natural repetitive rhythm.

When the unique neurological connection becomes *established*, healing Chi energy travels through the spinal column into the hypothalamus and pituitary glands. This phenomenon is achievable by Ones who have Mastered extreme body *relaxation* and *breathing techniques* and have full body control to start and maintain this process.

When thus connected in full synchronicity, this energy movement process starts muscle contractions and simultaneously ignites a rapid sequential firing of brain neurons firing with extreme intensity, … as Chakra balancing occurs.

Human joys, holding rarely known proportions of erotic bliss and ecstasy, are experienced during this conscious / semi-conscious / delirious state. Full body and mind sensations during the process combined with Love vibrations and healings are inwardly passed with intention to organs within the body. Energies are also passed to and from the Ethers during this process, little-known to Western Earthly World residents. Experiencing this state is a *unique incarnated Human phenomenon, one* of *Being fully Human*!

While this *alchemical transmutation* is occurring, both mental and physical sensations are keenly experienced.

Multiple sets of energy waves can continue for many Earth-minute durations and then repeat. Heightened energy waves pass upward through the head and scalp into the Crown Chakra, pleasingly stimulating scalp areas. Then, leaving the Human body, the ultimate destination of this euphoric / erotic energy stream is returned back into the Ethers and to Spirit from whence it originally emanated ... a reverse lightening rod of sorts. The circuit is complete. The entire Spiritual Realm can have awareness of this uniquely rare returning Human energy connection, freely streaming back to the Heavens. A completed circuit, if you will, directly linking Human essence with the entire Ascended Realm.

  Without further amplification at this point, be aware that such a state of healing and Chakra balancing is available to those of you who can call it forth for integration *into your overall Garden Weeding process.*

༚༝

Mastery of Self-Monitoring

Mastering the ability and on-going practice to transform an old obsessive judgment-making habit into Observation is a quality needed for a consciousness to attain *continued* residence in the 5th Dimension.

If this be your choice, you will make 'Weeding Your Garden' a top priority in the days and nights, weeks, and months ahead along your life stream journey, My Dearest Ones.

Although an oversimplification, I AM offering you a new way of Being, with a new technique of *observing* and healing a persistent Ego-judgment pattern ... or patterns of judgments in the making, 'loading up' so to speak. (Master chuckles ... hhmmmm hmmm).

A vigilant *self-monitoring action* will be invaluable to make you *aware that you are making a judgment when this is so*.

Consider this advanced self-Regulating process I offer very carefully. If you Master it, your evolutionary *progress and your Grand Process* will be infinitely accelerated ... if you have the fortitude and courage.

Nota bene! This purification is among the *most difficult and challenging of processes* in Human evolvement!

This tells you the importance of the internal preparations of which I speak!

Observation Dynamics

For ease of understanding and clarity, We have below a *Judgment Barometer*. The terms 'Good' and 'Bad' are connected to the barometer. Beware that these two generic terms also include less obvious and more subtle energies, often surrounding them *with somewhat disguised or obscure judgmental inferences, references, colors, and tones, etc.*

Read on carefully, My Dear Ones, ... the following may inspire you to connect the dots of this entire process, *'Weeding your Garden'*.

The idea of using *'Good' and 'Bad' energies* as *descriptives* is meant to distinguish between these opposite generics, *common labels* of Judgment.

In Human life, 'Good and Bad' carry meanings that hold polarized energies, *in* this context of consciousness, *(without confusion with the separate laws of physics)*. *These consciousness labels of separation hold* a 'position' or a 'belief' for example, ... that purports to carry within a judgment or opinion. **

However, in contrast, the energy of an *Observation* is meant to be free from the energies of 'Good' and 'Bad', ... and their inferences, ... maintaining a neutral position

with <u>no</u> emotional spin, <u>no</u> stigma of opinions, <u>no</u> labels, and *<u>no</u>* investment in beliefs ... and with <u>no</u> inflammatory polarizations attached.

A purified Observation, thusly <u>nonpolarized</u>, opens space to then embrace freely the 'What is of the Truth'.

With the bridge of 'The Truth' in place, ... as a trusted common denominator among Humans of Earth, ... All Humanity is empowered to vibrationally merge into the Higher vibration of ONENESS, a Divine Truth of the Cosmos ... w*ithout the opposition and conflict of Ego-separation ... separation so blatantly evident and terminally threatening now to the continued existence of your Earthly civilization!   Are you listening?*

** *'Polarized' is used here to distinguish opposites in a <u>Human consciousness context</u> and not with any reference to positive and negatively charged particles, protons and electrons, within the laws of Earthly physics, outside of this discourse.*

A Judgment Barometer

A barometer of measurement is available for you, … to observe the *frequency* that your Ego may simply revert to judging something to be categorically 'GOOD' OR 'BAD'. 👀

<mark>This is <u>your</u> litmus test!</mark> A useful rule of thumb, you might say.

  The JUDGMENT BAROMETER illustrates choice making patterns of a consciousness living in Separation, far apart from Oneness, … where All things are connected. And yes, the Human condition of Mankind's Ego separation is clearly distinct from Earthly Duality, an energy included by Spirit in the Earth School curriculum.

  To facilitate your Human understanding, … let Us herein refer to a very basic fundamental clarification, with *perspective* included.
  Read carefully!

'Good and Bad' are Man-made concepts! In contrast, the Cosmos is exemplary of ONENESS … where all things are Divinely. merged … without attached judgmental labels or stigma. Consequently, in Truth, there is no Cosmic 'Good and Bad'.   Read on.

Beware again, that broad judgments of 'Good and Bad' can carry *more subtle words and energies* that would cleverly disguise this broad label for an Observation, and nonetheless carry the fundamental meaning and intention of 'Good and/or Bad' as a Judgment!

Language itself carries its own scepter of deceit.

As you diligently self-observe your thinking patterns during this process of Purification and Change, … and for the remainder of this lifetime, … BEWARE of this:

> **When your Judgment Barometer reveals 'Good / Bad' and like labels and evaluations, … YOU are marching in Judgment Territory!**

OBSERVATION DYNAMICS
EXPANDED

The content of this book and of this entire process comprise an advanced Earth School course in Human awakening.

And for certain, full awakening is a process of a Human lifetime!

We Above are leading you to develop skills to navigate Third Dimensional challenges, and thereby to turn a bowl of sour lemons into a bowl of delectable lemonade. Capisce?

Developing your awareness and sklls to accurately perceive the *difference* between judgment and Observation is the root of this process. Your manifestation abilities are on the line, Folks.

A keen perception of your thoughts, feelings emotions, and sensations is a grand part of Being fully Human. The education here is about your choices about how you process these choices.

A *welcoming of your perceptions* into the *domain of Observation* is an enlightened manner of processing the inflow ... of 'What is"... and hence an embrace of the Truth.. Whereas, a choice of Ego to process perceptions with their patterns of Judgment leads you into the trap of Ego-separation vs. Unity. Look at your World of separation!

> <u>The giant chasm</u> between Observation and Judgment is as wide as your Grand Canyon!
> And there is no High-wire suspension midpoint for you to claim or hang on to, Folks. You are either standing on one side or the other!

And ... be heartened and encouraged, that the inflow of emotions I refer to have no immediate requirement to be *resolved per your evaluations and conclusions and opinions*, but rather they can be given space to dwell in the 'What is" of the moment. Eventually, Masters of this process learn to Love the Truth as it comes in to them! A peaceful surrender of sorts, blends you with the 'What is', with acceptance, and not necessarily an endorsement but a recognition thru perception.

Train yourself to recognize the <u>characteristics of judgments</u> that label, opinionize, Good/Bad colorings, etc., that so easily separate you from

your fellow man, bringing you into disunity, conflict, and disharmony.

Can you see that when your judgment 'monkeys around with the purity of 'what is', that you have deviated from the Truth of the moment by <u>adding your own embellishments</u>, spins, evaluations ?

'Ego seldom has an appetite for the Truth'!
If you choose, you can easily be stuck with a lifetime of judgment and separation. Your choice!

Honoring the <u>Integrity of Truth</u> can be viewed akin to honoring the integrity of your agreements, My Dear Ones.   Consider this. Can you appreciate the Freedom integrity can bring?

Lastly here, consider an example of Observation versus Judgment: EXAMPLE

'It is raining'   <u>OBSERVATION</u>

'It is raining   heavily   <u>JUDGMENT</u>
                 slightly
                 HARD
                 Forever
                 cats and dogs!
                 And, ……… .bla bla bla..

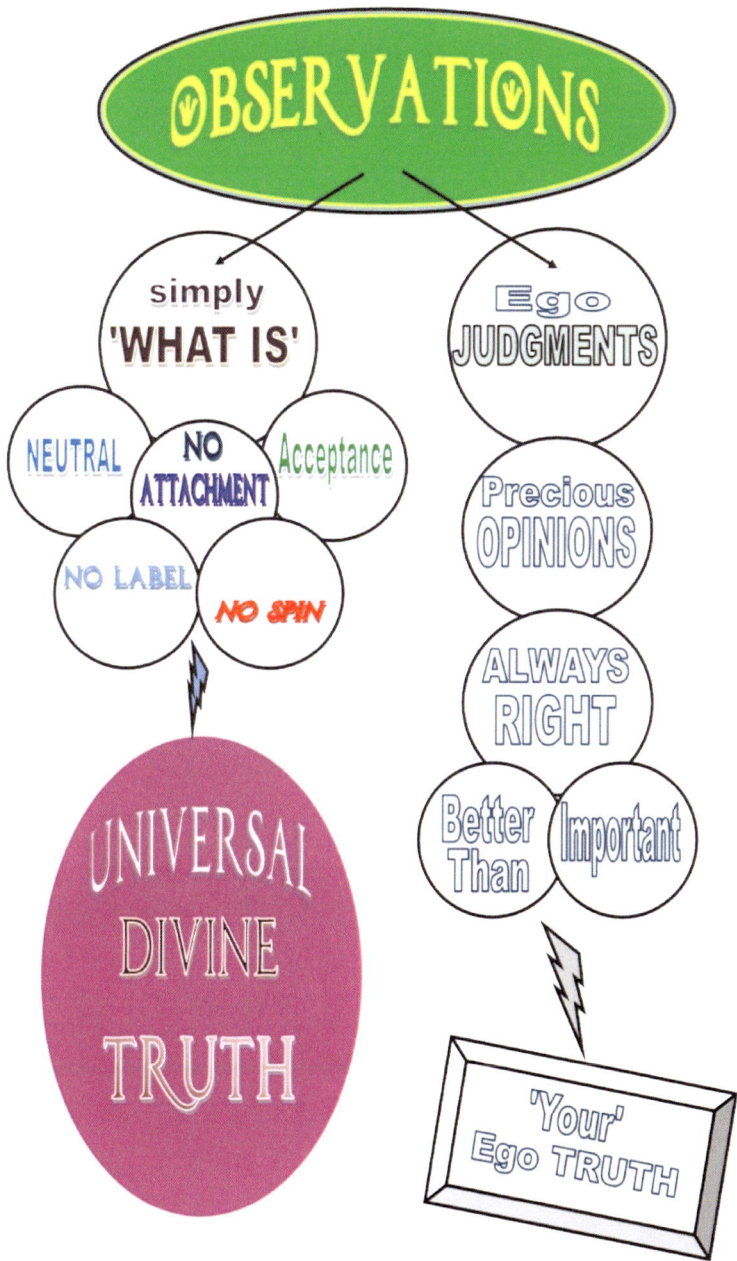

OBSERVATIONS

simply 'WHAT IS'

NEUTRAL
NO ATTACHMENT
Acceptance
NO LABEL
NO SPIN

UNIVERSAL DIVINE TRUTH

Ego JUDGMENTS

Precious OPINIONS

ALWAYS RIGHT

Better Than
Important

'Your' Ego TRUTH

The Pivotal Challenge of Change

With the foregoing *resources* in mind and hopefully *in practice*, I now proceed with the *external healing*. Let Us further examine the judgment pattern.

In contrast to the obvious continuing *habitual reactionary behavior* and *consequent judgment pattern*, … there is a pivotal alternative choice at hand for an aware consciousness.

Ripe opportunities surface when inevitable feelings and emotions are triggered and pop up on your radar screen, … on your mental computer monitor, so to speak, (Master chuckles … hmmmm hmmm.

I interject a digital flavor occasionally, to relate more vividly to you technology-obsessed Ones, sometimes turned from heartful to digital, and often glorified in binary notation, ha ha ha ha. Yes, I confess, … I am at times extra tickled enough to laugh at My own jokes. Once you become sufficiently evolved, you will be able to laugh along with Me!

You may want to take a good look at your current *personal judgment Barometer, as a progress bar throughout this healing process.* I AM referring to the barometer heretofore mentioned, indicating the *frequency* of categorized and labeled 'good and bad' Ego-judgments that you make.

Note that the degree of your progress can be equated to the increased level *of personal FREEDOM that you are newly experiencing as you progress.* Read on my fine Friends.

To be certain, Purification of consciousness does deliver abundant rewards toward the quality of your life as a Human, Dear Ones.

Accessing and holding a higher vibration gives birth to countless synchronicities that enormously enrich your Earth life, along with your ongoing full range of Human experience. I speak now of a delicious energy potential ... ultimately your new Freedom that awaits, ... a magnificent reward which follows the Mastery of this process healing.

Awareness Amplification

Heed awareness of your Ego-judgment barometer, indicating when you habitually <u>label judgments,</u> and lay them into a broad sweeping category of 'Good or Bad'. The *frequency* or *<u>infrequency</u>* of this judgment appearance will indicate your progress in Changing ... or Not, ... of re-wiring the old mental habit pattern.

  To amplify further, ... be clear that throughout this process of change, you are meant to *<u>continue experiencing,</u> ... without blocking, ... your own personal full spectrum of feelings and emotions*. Note the Light Body Diagram.

  The spectrum may include the pleasant-unpleasant, pleasing or not pleasing. positive-negative, nice or not nice, helpful - not helpful, wise - foolish, fast - slow, wet - dry, hot - cold, rich - poor, threatening- nonthreatening, fearful - non-fearful, beautiful - ugly, etc. etc.

Bear in mind that an Observation simply depicts 'what is'.

Observations carry no further labels.

Added Qualifications as Good and Bad, etc. are products of your Ego Judgments ... for which you are paying a high ransom!

Judgments are Weeds in your Garden. Humanity, collective and individual, has *unwittingly* been roped into a *judgment tradition*, becoming continuously entrapped as its victim!

The behavior of the Collective ironically entraps *you* individually, ... by the Collective's strong tradition! ... **if you continue to allow it!**

Your moment of Choice, for Change Dear Ones

Seize this *existential opportunity* to cleanse Your consciousness and belief system.

The Judgment Trap

Notice within yourself, … have you allowed feelings and emotions such as these earlier mentioned <u>to remain as Observations?</u>   **OR**   have you *proceeded to* <u>Judge and Label them</u> in your consciousness as fundamentally 'Good or Bad'? Opening Ego doors?

'Let you not always dignify your experience as the absolute Truth of the matter'.

Ponder this, if you dare.

<u>Am I OBSERVING</u>   or   <u>**JUDGING**</u>

<u>Your Choice for this transmutation.</u>

<u>Pure and simple, Folks!</u>

.

Extracting the Weeds

Together, We are re-programming your thinking pattern that holds you captive in Ego- separation because of an old judgment-making habit, yes? Purification is waiting … for you to extract these weeds, clean up your Garden, and to prevent further weed poppings-up, … for the remainder of this natural lifetime!

Realize now, **the Judgment trap** holds not only you … but millions of others, … captive to *personal collections of judgments (belief system) that* predominantly *separate you from each other*, … from your fellow Man, and at times from caring for one another, and from Being in Oneness with the All of All.

Again, … here is a fundamental: 'Good and/or Bad' does not exist … it is an Earthly man-made illusion, … it pervades Human behavior throughout your World!

If you rightfully claim to be 'awake and aware', this Truth will be abundantly clear to you.

Furthermore, if you stand in the man-made illusion of thinking in terms of 'Good and Bad', the *Judgment Trap confines you* to the lower vibration sector of the 3rd Dimension, … lacking the Freedom I describe, … blocking your potential entry into *the Beloved 5th Dimensional House of Higher Healing and Unconditional Love.*

In Higher Dimensions reached after 5th Dimensional Healing is complete, 'Good and Bad' and the judgment that sources these labels, … do not exist. Further, in *Atlantis at its height*, judgments to support good-bad polarity were unknown in the culture!

ॐ

Re-boot your Consciousness

Y ou have a ripe opportunity here to make *clooseable change* as you engage in this transformation, ... a mammoth change that will 're-boot' your consciousness into a higher Octave. Re-booting your consciousness is spoken figuratively here to resonate with computer oriented Ones who can appreciate re-booting to the factory reset, as the Creator intended for Human consciousness, ... a <u>default setting</u>, … that re-installs 'Truth' into Humanity leading to ONENESS, characterized by Joy.

This choice for change of consciousness is preparatory for entry into the 5th Dimension, Folks! … if this be your carrot.

<u>Ultimately</u>, merging *your* Unconditional Love into Oneness is the essence of Divine Ascension, for which this dissertation training is an intended essential key.

When you finally embody this energy and its aligned perspective, you will be on your way, walking along the high road into the Light.
❤️ ❤️ 🌈

Alright!

This takes us full circle, Folks. When you internalize the foregoing and *integrate* the knowledge into practice with all of its tentacles, you shall have become present to this advanced healing process I bring today.

I fully acknowledge, this feat of Change is easier said than done!
In certain respects, We Above would find this transformation process to be Super-Human!

And; when you bring this to Mastery, You shall be among the Extraordinary, with Worldly and Cosmic
Soul recognition alike … of achieving excellence in the Earth School curriculum!
You will then have my highest commendation and praise, My Fine Feathered Friends!

Connect the Dots below!

117

.

Consciousness Perspectives
Above and Below

Creator

Ascended Masters

Your **Soul-Self**

Your **Consciousness**

Life Experiences

Life's Lessons

Your Ego

Your Belief System

Saint Germain Through Iah Rahn Ananda 06-19

<u>Decrees</u>

   To further assist you in navigation this advanced process, Decrees are included here at the outset. These are intended to assist you in stabilizing your energy and centering your Spiritual alignment. Use Our Decrees when you are between thoughts, taking a break, deep breathing, before or after meditation, or perhaps during idle minded moments. Memorize them for ready reference, always at your fingertips. Your diligence of use is an *indication of your level of Self-love in action*, here and as always.

   In years to come, you will be grateful for Decreeing! Repeating these short Decrees three times in sequence will assist in achieving their purpose for this process and in your future as an evolving Human.

   Memorized and often Self-repeated, … morning, noon, or night, … and <u>prior</u> to Meditation if you like, Decrees will serve you well to over-shine otherwise Ego-dominated thoughts and moments that <u>can invade an idle mind</u> … especially 'when troubles come not in single spies but in battalions!

Violet Flame Decree

I AM the Violet Flame
In Action in Me Now
I Am the Violet Flame
To Light Alone I Bow
I Am the Violet Flame
In Mighty Cosmic Power
I Am the Violet Flame
Shining Every Hour.

I AM the Violet Flame
That Saturates Me Now
I AM the Violet Flame
Here to Show Me How
I Am the Violet Flame
In Mighty Cosmic Power
I Am the Violet Flame
Shining Every Hour.

I AM the Violet Flame In Action in Me Now
I Am the Violet Flame, To Light Alone I Bow

I Am the Violet Flame Blazing Like a Sun
I Am the Light of God Freeing Everyone.

The Holy Presence

I AM that I AM
I AM that I AM
Oh GOD I know that I AM that I AM.

I AM I AM Beholding ALL
Mine Eye is single as I Call
Oh Raise Me Now and Set Me Free
Thy Holy Presence Now to BE.

Repeat 3 times, ending with

Om (A-u-m) m

Mmmm
Mmm

mmmmmm.

Awareness of Your Judging

A**lright!**

I AM referring to your awareness of when *you are actually making a judgment* **when** *you are making a judgment!* When this awareness becomes real to you, you have a choice. And that is to refine your process, **… to shift your judgments into observations of neutral energy, where you have No ultimate position, No investment, No positive or negative spin included, No attachment to holding anything as labeled *'good or bad'.***

The Cosmos is One,
and its integral parts are not sorted out as 'good or bad'. Capiche?
Now translate this into 'As Above so below.'
Are you with me?
Can you connect these dots?

As Shakespeare, it might interest you to know, I optimistically nudged Humanity some 200+ years ago to make a fundamental change in behavior, to recognize that:

" *There is no GOOD OR BAD, it is only your thinking that makes it so*"

Applying this axiom of Truth and purifying your Human behavior into Oneness, Unconditional Love, and Freedom … will act to serve you well, *if you will have it!!*

To fully engage in this process, Humans must first become *aware of their behavior … in real time.* Your capability for timely awareness of judgment making now becomes a critical key to *achieving the higher vibration you may seek to Rise Above the Third Dimension.*

Yes, to be sure, the option of free-will choice comes into play throughout this refinement.

You may continue with *your judgments as your Ego may choose, or you may use your free-will to choose a new enlightened path toward an Extraordinary life.*

∂◌∂

The 'What Is' Opening

When you proceed to alter your judgment patterns of 'Good and Bad labeling', so to speak, there appears a magnificent *opening for you to become fully present about 'what is'.*
Learn, if you wish, to enthusiastically engage in your full experiences of life and simultaneously cease the limiting judgments of separation.

  Being open and surrendered and satisfied to intake the Truth of 'what is' is a magnificent escalation in your own process. Your *awareness* of which I speak then becomes a fundamental Keystone in your arch of personal evolvement.

  With this awareness in place, your life is expanding, becoming surrendered to the 'what is of TRUTH'. With Truth in your grasp, you are empowered to walk across into the uncharted territory of *Automatic* Observation.

  Thus positioned, you are a *candidate* to Rise Above to advance from Ordinary to BE EXTRAORDINARY!   🙏🌈❤️!

About the 'What Is'

When the full meaning of 'What is' strikes a Human consciousness, the impact can appear to be abruptly startling and stare you in the face <u>or</u> at times, simply strike you as a minor ho-hum event of no apparent consequence.

Regardless, Humans are typically drawn to *incessantly think about and to alter the naked 'what is' by attaching their judgments, … without awareness of the consequences, …* without conscious pause to accept the <u>*Truth*</u> *of 'what* is' in the moment.

<u>First, We have the whole egg.</u> That is 'what is'. Once the whole egg is cracked, opened and put to the fire, and scrambled, … there would appear to be a new 'what is', … as opposed to 'what was'. The egg is now scrambled, and that cannot be changed! Reverting back to the whole egg is no longer *a changeable* option. The new circumstance is *now* simply 'what is', and Wisdom would endorse this recognition.

<u>A Human's opinion</u> of denial and/or wish for a different outcome cannot unscramble the egg. This scrambled egg is 'what is'. Yet, Humans commonly add their reactions, emotions, thoughts, and feelings <u>as judgment</u> about

'what is', … intending to modify it or give it color, … rather than merely OBSERVING it, … and by so doing they superimpose various forms of 'good and/or bad' based judgments, … which attempts to *alter the TRUTH of 'what is' with added colors of Ego-separated-judgment!*

Now, … the One who judges is *caught in the judgment trap* and stuck with the illusions and burdens of a consciousness out of Alignment.

This act of judging introduces varying energies of different perspectives, differences of opinion, labels, disagreements and more , … leading to Human separation … from the simple Truth that we nonetheless have a scrambled egg … as a 'what is'!

Divergence from the Truth, … with Humanity's automatic default tradition of rampant Ego-separation behavior in full force, … is *Mankind's Cosmic-disconnect signature behavior,* … of abandoning *the path of Truth leading to Oneness* ... to create Harmony, Love, Care for One Another, and Abundance, … a Blessing that has *eluded* Humanity for eons of Earth time past. Your civilization's time is running out! This is the *extistential* moment to act! This starts with healing *individual consciousnesses*! *That would be You Weeding*

 your Garden!

With an activated critical mass of Enlightened Human consciousness in free-will swing, this current sad signature behavior is truly *changeable* into a new and brilliant recognition of 'what is' TRUTH in full Divine alignment for the highest and best well-Being of All Mankind!

Your inspired engagement in this transformative process of Weeding Your Garden, *Change and Purification*, is the future of Humanity!

Saint Germain

137

Duality is a Reality

*U*ntil you agree to practice the pivotal
awareness as I have earlier highlighted,
... confusion of the moment, pain, and
suffering may take a front seat in your life
journey, as you would insist upon swimming in
the Ego infested, difficult Third Dimensional
soup surrounding an ORDINARY Human life
on the karmic wheel.

In My recent book, 'Duality In Perspective', you
will find a plethora of clarifying Wisdom that
you shall now need to fully embrace this
process of Weeding Your Garden, Dear Ones.

Duality is an often Humanly misunderstood
reality that Humans *confuse* with the good-
bad, nice and not nice, positive-negative Third
Dimensional conglomeration, ... mixed in with
Human emotions, reactions, and judgments.
You will need to acquire this work about
Duality and absorb its contents to sort this out
and to fully embrace *Cleansing and Purifying*.

Embracing Duality

FREEDOM

Alignment

Self-correction

Non-Judgment

Choice

Surrender

Perspective

Awareness and Focus

CIRCUMSTANC**e**

As you may observe by now, … as Saint Germain, I have sourced over a fifteen Earth year time span prior to this transmission, … a massive body of Spiritual Wisdom in a series of *interrelating* books.

This Ascended Master Library of Wisdom has been manifested, along with My Blessed Earth Partner Lah Rahn Ananda, into a Series of now Eight books … that are Divinely linked together, *overlapping* into a fully integrated, comprehensive body of Masterful Realm Wisdom for *timely Human consumption*.

Typically a new work, as this that I now source today, will require your reference to one or more of My preceding series books, … enabling you to embrace the full essence of the topic at hand, and to open doorways for your Mastery.

Such is the case here. *Duality In Perspective*, and *Rising Above, A Journey into Higher Dimensions*, and *The Saint Germain Chronicles Collection, A Journey into Practical Spirituality* … are all <u>*supplementally needed for you to tackle an advanced integrated process as :*</u>
Weeding Your Garden, Purification in Action.

These works are Amazon available, search: Gordon Corwin II, or saintgermainbooks.com for Amazon link .

Treat yourself to these works as Self-love gifts from yourself to yourself, gifts of a lifetime!

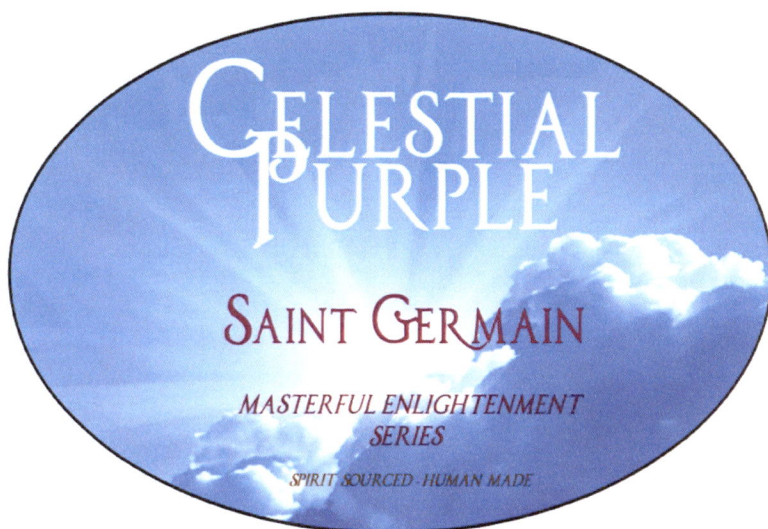

Alright! Moving on.

Awareness and Change

THIS PIVOTAL EVOLUTIONARY CHANGE OF CONSCIOUSNESS IS NOT FOR THE FAINT OF HEART!

G iving up your *attachment* to a deeply embedded habit of making thousands of judgments per day ... and allowing some of these to morph into steadfast opinions in your belief system ... is a mammoth endeavor of AWARENESS, CHANGE, and PURIFICATION.

For Humans, animals, and plants alike, as I pointed out earlier, Change is a major challenge and can appear to be extremely *confrontive*. In Truth, even seemingly small changes can be shocking to the Human nervous system. We Bless you with Our compassion.

Change of habit can be extremely difficult for some, ... this particular Change for Purification is near the top of the challenge list. Success in this regard will require the ultimate *commitment* on your part to apply unwavering discipline, perseverance, and persistence, and self-monitoring for you to prevail.

Lacking any of these qualities, We ABOVE observe HUMANS to remain stuck in the Third Dimensional Vibration of Human life … and although with a fair share of Earthly beauty to enjoy, … also stuck, inextricably intertwined in this characteristic Ego-saturated, dense morass, muck. and mire which you have no doubt experienced by this time in your life. If this vibration be your status, how has that worked out for you so far?

HEALING YOUR JUDGMENTS INTO ONENESS

CREATOR

ONENESS

COMPASSION

LOVE

JUDGMENTS

YOUR LIFE'S CIRCUMSTANCES

Saint Germain 02-2023

151

As you will see at the conclusion of this transmission, I have appended one of My formerly published *works* which will greatly assist you in *tackling the* Change *facing you here and now.*

The name of this former Transmission is 'FRIEND OF CHANGE'. Many have found this to be positive reinforcement along their paths. I pray you will add your name to the list. When you have completed your reading and study of *Weeding Your Garden*, *be Blessed to* read on, and incorporate *Friend of Change* into your process and your life.

Your Ripe Opportunity

Alright! In particular today, I address for your edification this clear focus of becoming aware about <u>when</u> you are engaged in Ego judgment-making, … and that *<u>you become thusly Aware of this in that instant</u>!*

<u>Start to focus your attention, for example, upon a certain reaction taking place about a certain something that is happening to you in real time.</u>

<u>Now observe yourself, … observe, not judge!</u>

When this happens, there is a ripe and ready opportunity to recognize a situation that has arisen … and is in front of you, … a chance to feel whatever emotion is there, and to give yourself *loving permission to observe yourself* and <u>any possible trigger that has been activated</u>.

And next, <u>make the self-correction</u> of replacing your *judgment patterns, newly devoid of any judgment or any discomfort about 'what is' Being what is!* *This would then be neutral.*

As a side-note here for you, … again, please refer to My extensive and exhaustive descriptions of emotional

processing in My book *'The Saint Germain Chronicles Collection, A journey into practical Spirituality', Amazon published in 2016.* *If you are sincere about moving into the 5th Dimension, this book is a must have and a must read and a must understand work of Divine Wisdom, …* <u>*to forward your process.*</u>

<u>**At this point, for simplicity,**</u> **let us observe an incoming thought and consider: is this something 'I like or perhaps something I do not like'?**

This distinction is an expansion and yet a more subtly expressed refinement of *viewing something as 'good or bad'.*

With these two polar extremes now in mind … connected to this emotion … you then have a *choice* **to record in your belief system, as 'I like -   I don't like   this' emotion,** <u>*and*</u> *its likely consequent* <u>*judgment*</u> *Or Not* *and* *nonetheless filing away the emotion as* *observation into a space of* **'it is what it is' .**

In other words, this removes your emotional spin from the risk of a triggered reaction leading to possible judgment and opinion to follow.

The Litmus Test!

**As a highlight of your Ripe Opportunity,
We now come to:
Surrendering, Acceptance, and
Alignment**

I would call this the neutral zone. This newly created vibration embraces *Surrender*, including an element of acceptance, as you will see.

Holding this space is now key to lead you into Divine alignment.

When you move your polarized energy reactions into 'it is what it is', you are surrendering to TRUTH ... separate from opinion, ... and separate from Your Truth, if that be different.

Here, TRUTH *excludes your preferences, your judgments' or your opinions and hopefully your reactions, transmuting you into an entirely new octave of consciousness.*

At this point you have succeeded in *rebalancing* yourself into a neutral zone, where judgment does not have power over you, ... into a neutral zone where JUDGMENT No Longer Lives!

HARMONY

In Human terms,

Reality is relative.

You may *blend* these realities if you wish.

However,

The Truth is absolute.

You cannot *bend* the Truth.

A secret of Human Harmony holds a

conscious distinction between the

Absolute and   the Relative.

Can you See?

Can you see how embracing the ==TRUTH== likely moves you out of your precious Ego-saturated, opinionated positions, … your earlier reactions based on *Ego-recorded past experiences* , … your precious beliefs about certain things, your family's traditions of approaching certain things, … and how Truth can move you away from a 3-D societally accepted judging standard that, in this case, is a *man-made trap of Human illusio*n?

Ponder this tidbit, Lads, and Lassies.
Without realizing and knowing of this trap, you will continue to wear your blinders, … to be stuck unwittingly swimming in the soup of 3rd Dimensionnel vibration. Do I have your attention?

Ego and Illusion

C ontinuing down the road of constant judgment-making, … *although ironically endorsed by societies upon Earth across your Earth globe,* … is a sad journey to further entrapment in a separated Third Dimensional Ego soup offering difficulty to stay afloat.

  Until you leap over this Ego hurdle of judgment-making, … you will continue to mingle and waddle in the 3rd Dimensional energies of the Earth World where you now live! The Earth School has much more to offer you than being stuck swimming in the Human illusion, such as the 3-D Judgment trap. 5th, 7th, and 9th Dimensional Domains lay ahead for the dedicated. ... offering Harmony, Abundance, and Health, with Joy, Truth and Love.

  In all fairness to you for your progress, I must point out a relevant and recent book I have released, along with My Beloved Earth Partner Lah Rahn Ananda. In this dissertation, and in many of those to follow, you will note My frequent references to *distinctions between DIMENSIONS.* For many of you, this deserves clarification.

Therefore, I would recommend for you to immediately acquire and study the contents of this new book entitled RISING ABOVE, A Journey into Higher Dimensions. Amazon available. Gift yourself with this gem of Wisdom, … for you shall need its contents to fully embrace the importance of transmuting your judgment-making habit.

Can you wrap your arms around this process and actually begin to apply it? *Getting started* often meets resistance.

It is said that 'the cause for change is crisis'. Mark My words about this existential moment of choice for Humanity, Folks!! The Global Human consciousness is a crisis and it must be changed. It starts with the individuals and ideally morphs into a critical mass to then manifest Aligned collective change. This individual would be you.

Can you embrace My words, as *your* new process of transmuting JUDGMENTS into OBSERVATIONS, rather than further indulging *in manufactured judgments* that morph into opinions and find their way into your belief system, … only to require you to later purge them out of your belief system with more difficulty at a later date?

Moving beyond the illusionary Ego-attraction to judgment-making requires a stark awakening about the Truth, Folks.

When Ones open up to their visceral attraction to the Truth, and then experience the rewards of Truth, they have already accessed a new quantum of Light. Once in the Light, there is no turning back and a voracious hunger for the Truth dances to stage center!

In essence, Ones who Master this healing process become **Truth Seekers** at Heart, a proclivity once acquired never to be lost.

THE TRUTH

DIG DEEPLY FOR REWARDS
OF THE TRUTH, WHERE
EARTHLY ILLUSION
FADES INTO THE DUSK ...

AND JOYS OF FRESHLY
FOUND FREEDOMS BECOME
YOURS FOREVER".

The Caress

'A Divining Soul forever pulsates with unbounded ecstasy and delight ... in sweet caress of countless Light-filled Cosmic waves of Truth.'.

Truth Seekers elevate to Truth Holders

Advancing along your Spiritual path, you shall eventually discover and embrace the undeniable role of the Truth.

Standing in the full presence of the Truth opens your visceral connection to the expansive wholeness of Cosmic Wisdom.

With this vision, it is clear to see the key position held by the naked Truth, inextricably surrounded by the phenomenon of 'What is'.

Despite Ego temptations, Ones awake and aware hold this placement in the highest regard.

Disappointments aside, ... neither embellishments, modifications, nor negotiations will alter 'The Truth'.

173

Alluring illusions of flawed and superimposed Ego-judgment energy have no power to blur nor stain the purity of the Truth!

Truth Seekers destined to become Forever *Truth Holders* as they escalate into higher Dimensions, need have a keen awareness that Humans have Domain over Truth bridging *to Cosmic Oneness!*
Behold and cherish the bridge of Truth leading into Oneness, *in your hands for the taking*, individually and collectively...
If you will have it!

Higher Dimensions

Once you Master this process of **Weeding your Garden,** Change and Purification, ... to consciously experience feelings and emotions, recognizing the temptations of judgment-making actions teetering on the threshold, ... to consciously rebalance into the 'what is' of the Truth ... accepting and being *satisfied and consistent* with this choosing, ... and making a new *habit* of this process, ... <u>then</u>, ... I pray pray pray you will be *otherwise eligible* to Rise Above ... as a remembrance of your Loving Divine-self.

Your Soul beckons for this remembrance now, especially in these Earth times of Global and individual separation, and during *this incarnation* era of your life stream.

Merging this <u>Grand Purification Process</u> imbedded in your full consciousness opens the door for an expanded perspective of who you are becoming, ... with essential *pieces of the enlightenment puzzle* taking their rightful places.

This illustration expands upon My words.

GRAND PURIFICATION PROCESS
PIECES OF A PUZZLE

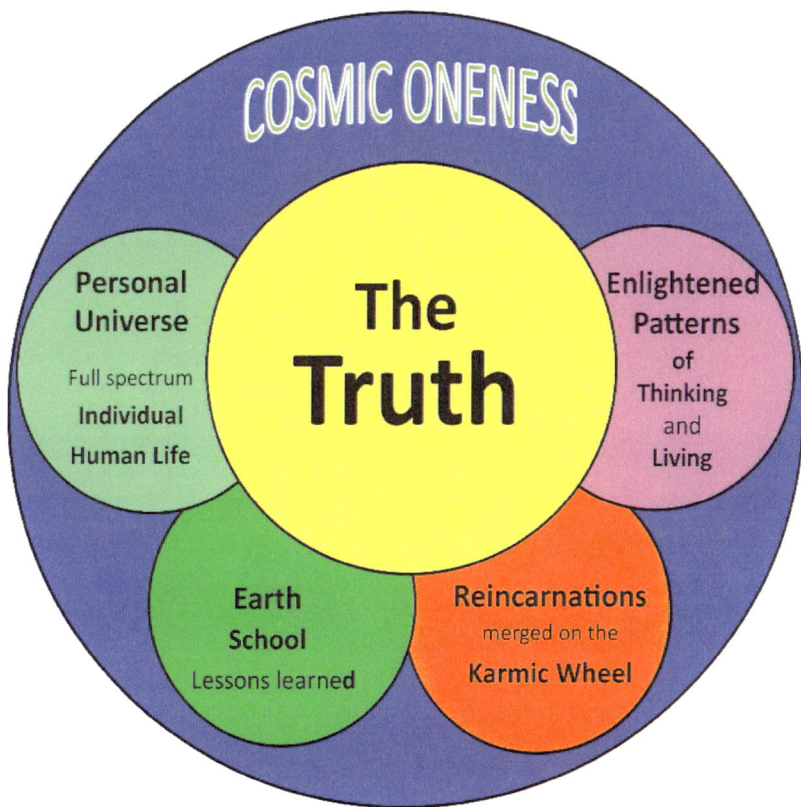

COSMIC ONENESS

The **Truth**

Personal Universe
Full spectrum
Individual
Human Life

Enlightened Patterns of Thinking and Living

Earth School
Lessons learned

Reincarnations
merged on the
Karmic Wheel

Exchanging Judgments
for Observations

Here lies the core essence of Weeding your Garden.

This is a moment-by-moment discipline. You are shifting a life-long habit of Judging ... into a new *automatic habit* and life-long practice of consciously Observing and Witnessing. This is the transformation at hand. This is an essential purification needed to enable residence into the 5th Dimensional House of Higher Healing, simply and plainly stated. This new habit pattern, once Mastered, delivers you into a new and higher state of BEING.

Focus and concentrate keenly upon this very delicate process.

When thoughts enter your mind and linger, when sensations inflow and rest in your body, and mind, ... recognize their presence and make your choice to simply observe 'what is'.

181

<u>When you learn to repeatedly bypass
temptations to lapse into opinions born from
judgments, You have scored a personal
Victory! Congratulate yourself!</u>

A New Energy Shift

Inside your Auric Field, when this new discipline is learned and executed repeatedly, … moment by moment along your lifestream, … *you are elevating your vibration into an entirely new Octave.*

   The effect of this new energy field surrounding your Being is stunningly amazing, as you shall notice. Others may notice as well.

   When the heavy burden of thousand upon thousands of judgments is lifted, One feels a corresponding new Freedom, never before experienced. We observe Humans typically heaving a huge sigh of relief and beholding this new reality. New breathing patterns emerge, A sense of Peace and Well-being is also common at this point.

   Ones relate to Us Above that their perceived 'Beast of Burden' has been lifted from their

.

shoulders, oft into thin air! Some characterize these as their former demons.

Purified Auric Field

Experiencing a 5th Dimensional presence is truly an amazing event for a Human.
Enjoy the ride!

The 5th Dimension is an energetic Domain that *sources* healings of Love, Happiness, and Abundance infused healings with opportunities *leading to* integrate Joy, Awareness, and Unconditional Love into the mix.

ॐॐ

THE JOY
OF
BEING PRESENT

FOCUS ON YOUR
HEART

STOP <u>OVER</u>THINKING

LET GO OF
YOUR DOUBTS
FEARS
ASSUMPTIONS.
AND
SURRENDER TO YOURSELF
ABOUT 'WHAT IS'

ENJOY THE PEACE!

The Third Dimension and Above

As a candidate to live Above the 3-D consciousness, where some of you may now reside, You will potentially be empowered to *achieve and maintain* a higher vibration of 5th Dimensional level and potentially beyond. *Mastering <u>this process</u> is one of your tickets for entry through this doorway.* There is no compromise or negotiation of a *half-way consciousnes*s.

<u>As an additional positive reinforcement</u> for you to make this *key change in your Ego behavior*, your Higher-self will be delighted to know this:

Once judgment-making is exchanged for impartial neutral observation, keen, and awake and aware, ... You will be unbelievably exhilarated by a new sense of FREEDOM, that will knock your socks off.
Your Judgment Beast of Burden lives no longer.

This is the Ripe Opening I referred to at the start, Folks! Joy, Truth, and Love surround surrendered Ones that hover in the Higher Dimensions. I pray you shall enter these gates.

Take a glimpse below at certain energies that await in the *Seventh Dimension* of Human consciousness, My fine Feathered Friends. For different Humans they show up here in different ways, manifesting in varying degrees for different Humans along their paths.

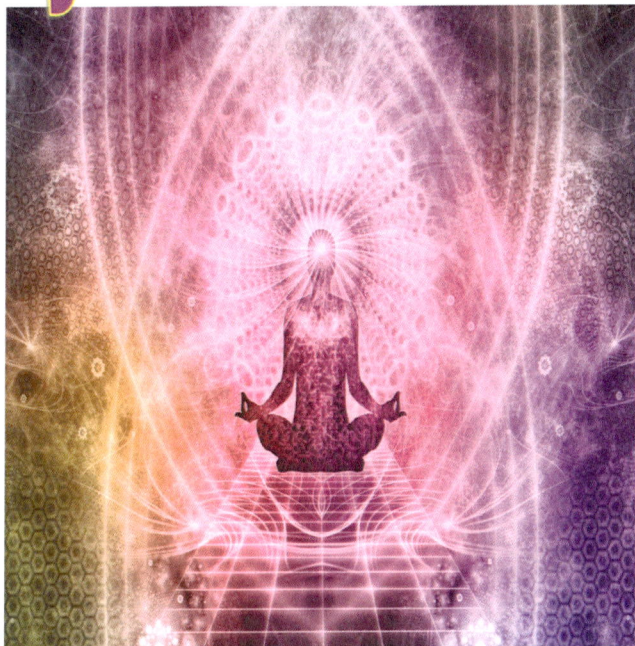

Joy Truth Love

Harmony Abundance Health

For graduates of this 'Grand Process of Purification', say goodbye to that *Beast of Judgment burden.* You shall then heave a grand sigh of relief! This burden of a lifetime will be lifted from your shoulders. You will be looking up to the Heavens in Gratefulness for the guidance you are receiving here and now.

Time will tell.

Gratitude

For some of you, Gratitude will become your middle name when you begin reaping the benefits of exchanging JUDGMENT-MAKING for OBSERVATION MAKING!

THIS ADVANCED PLANE OF CONSCIOUSNESS WILL UNBURDEN your Human life in ways you *have not dreamed of. This is a unique brand of FREEDOM of which I now speak.* It is far apart from 'traditional' perceptions of Freedom where, for example, you may no longer have a 'boss', you may have financial independence, less work, more pay, LESS CONFINEMENT, etc.

This FREEDOM is an upliftment of the Heart and Mind into a space of Well-being, Joy, Truth, Love, and Harmony that Divinely Graces surrendered Ones who Master this Grand Process of Purification.

If this be so for you, *your True Gratitude* will be recognized by Spirit Above and propel you onward with abounding *synchronicities.*

We Above receive your Gratitude with loving open arms. Gratitude is a catalyst for synchronicity to be showered upon you.

True Gratitude is a delicate energy,
justly adorned with the Highest-octave of
vibration emanating from the Human
Heart and from the Heart of Spirit itself.

ॐ॰ॐ

8

RISING ABOVE

In the 5th Dimension of Higher Healing, as I describe to you in My book RISING ABOVE, *A Journey into Higher Dimensions*, … you are hovering in a new and loving space of *consciousness* healing, a gargantuan leap in the Human experience. The 5th Dimensional vibration places you in a sterling new phase of your life, along with an ENLIGHTENED PERSPECTIVE about incoming events and circumstances, as they occur in real time … mixed with a fair share of Adversity, Love, Harmony and Abundance.

Let Us now take a step further, if you dare.

When Humans enter or take residence in the 5th Dimension of consciousness, We Above observe you beginning to connect the dots between Self-love, Conditional-love, … casual or romantic, ... and the *initial experience of Unconditional Love.* This is a glorious transformation sequence for the Ascended Realm to behold. 'Etherical clapping' can be heard afar on Alpha Centauri!! (Master chuckles … haaahammmmm).

Although uncommon in your Earth plane, *Unconditional Love* magnificently seats itself in the depths of a Human Heart. Ones desperately

striving for this experience … by taking a *determined* <u>*mental plunge*</u> *… in vain* … into imagined Unconditional-Love … end upside down in confusion and frustration. Their Egos victoriously insisting upon attaching and enforcing conditions upon their closely guarded *ration of mind-love-for-barter* … in quid pro quo fashion, … placing Unconditional-Love nowhere within reach!

The 5th Dimension of Higher Healing is your <u>gateway</u> to Ascended octaves of higher Heart-Love vibrations. Weeding Your Garden, Cleansing and Purification, is your integrative <u>process</u> to clear the path ahead.

Realize that as you *truly Rise Above* along your Spiritual journey, … 5th Dimension, hopefully 7th dimension, and perhaps 9th Dimension, you are in place to experience traversing the Golden Bridge of Unconditional-Love that Alchemically and Metaphysically connects to ONENESS.

IN this beautiful state of transfdormation, the view and perspective of your lifetime enrolled in the Earth School will be ironically *upended* into sharp *focus!* *(Master chucklesss again hhaahhmmmmmm0)*

Meanwhile, My Dearest Lads and Lassies, Our mission for this process is to elevate you to springboard into the 5TH Dimension and claim your entry ticket!

> Ones describe their entry into the 5th Dimension with a huge sigh of relief. They realize the vast quantities of life energies that have been previously sucked out of them to no avail, mind and body ... by an Ego-ridden life filled with judgments, opinions, being right, competition, placing blame, getting even, revenge, and a host of other draining 3-D Ego behaviors.

My following diagram illustrates the natural *unobstructed progression* of Human evolvement from the first Divine spark of an incarnating Human Being, overlayed with Earthly Beauty, Duality in Perspective, and Free-will mixed with Ego-consciousness, ... *progressing upward* to integrate with Love, Unity, Oneness and ultimately the Divine Mind. Enjoy this journey, My Dearest Ones.

This is you, … you are the Divine Spark of Human Beingness, remembering who you truly are during your Spiritual journey.

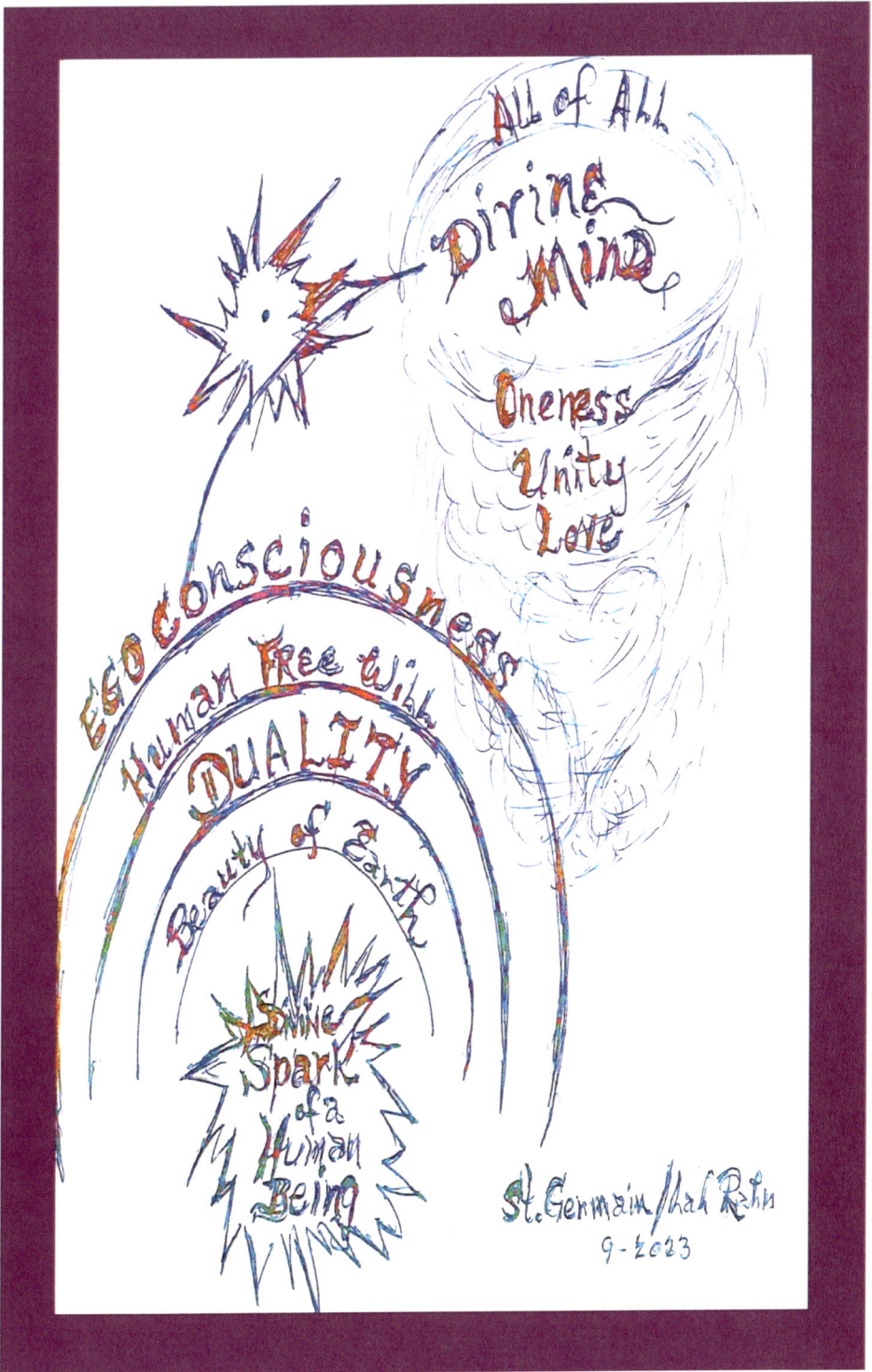

All of All

Divine Mind

Oneness
Unity
Love

Ego Consciousness
Human Free Will
DUALITY
Beauty of Earth

Divine Spark of a Human Being

St. Germain/hal Rahn
9-2023

209

Life Lessons are Teachers

Life's lessons realized are priceless gifts. <u>They introduce *possibilities to elevate your consciousness into the Light, using your life Events as the teachers.*</u>

Be cogently aware that you must deeply desire to make this gigantic leap from habitual ego-judgment, moving automatically into new habitual neutral observations of 'what is' and thereafter attaining your FREEDOM as One no longer living in separation.

Changing a lifelong habit will require your utmost attention, discipline, perseverance, self-observation, and self-monitoring, as I have afore mentioned and emphasized. Here, the <u>responsibility rests upon your shoulders.</u> Your task is to put this Wisdom in its rightful place.

Spiritual aspirants, Lightworkers, Chelas, and Devotees alike must massively rein in their Egos to make this gigantic forward leap! Ones content with halfway or status quo ridden efforts to walk this fine line …. will be sadly disappointed. … and remain strapped into The HUMAN CONDITION unhealed … read the results recorded in your Human history of this civilization upon Earth! This would be Humanity's <u>track record</u>, if you will.

ॐ

Motivation and Courage

YOU MUST TRULY WANT TO DO THIS !

If you have the courage to implement this healing I AM sourcing, ... into every moment of your life, and to persist in modifying reactive or opinionated emotions into *a surrendered place of 'it is what is',* ... *you will be passing muster* to potentially receive 5th Dimensional Vibrations beyond your wildest expectations, My Dear Ones.

For those *recalcitrant* Ones faint of Heart, entering the 5th Dimension is nothing more than an idle daydream. Your choice ...
Your life time.

I know that this courage is a lot to ask. We in Spirit are compassionate for you. After all, moment you reincarnated, you have been from the raised in a 3-D space where your Human world society standards of judgment are firmly implanted.
A staggeringly large number of these World

standards involve deeply embedded, time honored judgment practices in various ways.
See for yourself, analyze the standards 3-D society has set up for you, ... and yes, compounded with Spirit's placement of

DUALITY on Earth as part of the Earth
school curriculum.
I therefore leave you now with
My utmost compassion and Blessing, as you
navigate your Human path toward
Becoming the EXTRAORDINARY Being of
excellence that your Soul beckons you to BE!

Put My Loving Gift of today's Wisdom in to
practice if you will and come to distinguish
yourself as One who is RISING ABOVE, along
your Human destiny into higher Dimensions.

I leave you now with fondest Blessings,
My Dearest Ones
Until We shall meet again,

Saint Germain
with
Lah Rahn Ananda
Aka Gordon Corwin II

ACKNOWLEDGEMENTS

Once again, I Am overjoyed to acknowledge you who have contributed so much talent and Love to the Worldly Spiritual value of this book, *Weeding Your Garden, Cleansing and Purification.*

You generous Ones have graciously given your love, time, and ongoing support to the success to writing and publishing this book, using your own personality, unique creative talents and abilities, artistry, technical skills, financial resources, and much more.

Please know that YOU are most highly appreciated! Without your support, this book would not have been born as it is into life for all of those who would surround themselves with this advanced layer of Masterful Wisdom.

My heartful thanks goes out to each of you, with best wishes for your continued advancement along your Spiritual journey and in your varied careers of endeavor. I continue to send, along with Ascended Master Saint Germain, highest Blessings, admiration and love.

Lah Rahn Ananda
aka Gordon Corwin II

LLantar Chris Gulve, my longtime loyal friend and Spiritual Chela, for your inspiration and support to begin this eighth published book of channeled Wisdom dedicated to enlightening Human lives in those many vitally important facets of Weeding Your Garden. Your selfless and steady encouragement throughout the creation of this book, along with contributing most capable and diligent proof reading of the manuscript, has been of value beyond description. You are acknowledged with the greatest of appreciation, with many grateful thanks from both myself as the Author and Ascended Master Saint Germain and the Realm. Love and Blessings to you.

Proof reading services from: llantar@sbcglobal.net

Jossue Legaspi Aguirre, my Soul brother in this lifetime and Soul compadre over several past-lives, I salute you for your enthusiastic willingness to support the creation of my work with Spirit, while continuing with your own. Your consciousness and Soul have rapidly grown to be an extraordinary messenger of life's lessons dynamically delivered to the Author in real time during the channeling process of these many new books. You continue to gift quality experiences of value in friendship, comradery and adventure, many of which were and are so very inspirational in creating this work for Humanity. You have my Unconditional Love, brotherly friendship, and gratitude always.

Tim Yargeau, with special thanks for your kind and enthusiastic co-operation in applying your creative and very effective graphic design and photography skills, just when they were most needed! The results of your fine work, begun with the Saint Germain Chronicles Collection book project, greatly enhancing the true beauty of many graphic displays throughout the book as well.

Your many image creations were also used in Saint Germain's numerous new books including '*Victory For the Soul*, Relationships That Work, *Rising Above, Duality, Truth and Betrayal, True Com,passion, Manifestation Magic, Weeding Your Garden'*, and others which have been written and are yet unpublished. t.-yargeau@gmail.com

Marius Michael-George, for the most beautiful licensed, color images of your paintings, presenting likenesses of Ascended Masters Saint Germain and El Morya. Artwork © Marius Michael-George www.Mariusfineart.com

Dreamstime.com, for your print licensed permission to utilize graphic images that add so much to illustrate text, solely inside the book in various places, with imagination and beauty. Dreamstime.com

FCIT Florida Center for Instructional Technology, for the licensed use of your copyrighted, beautiful floral, ornate, and decorative capital letters to illustrate text, inside of the book. licensing@fcit.us

123RF Limited, for your beautiful graphic images, print licensed for Our use, adding so much illustrative vitality in various places, solely inside of the book. 123RF.com

Public Domain, for location of the Comte Saint Germain portrait, and the circa 1864 Charles Sindelar public domain original portrait image of Saint Germain. The Public Domain Review

❦❧

Friend of Change

Spoken by Ascended Master

𝔖𝔞𝔦𝔫𝔱 𝔊𝔢𝔯𝔪𝔞𝔦𝔫

A Channeled Live Dictation through Lah Rahn Ananda
Circa July 1998

This work was taped live during a public Sacred Life Gathering of Souls in Oceanside, California USA who came together in love and surrendered dedication to witness Spirit, hear their words, and feel the essence of the Ascended Masters speaking.

The Master speaking upon this occasion was Lord Saint Germain, Chohan of the Aquarian Age, delivering loving support to individuals dedicated to mastering their human lives in Divine alignment in *this* lifetime. Neither the audience nor the channel had prior knowledge of the message to come nor the subject which was to be addressed.

Many were surprised and taken that day by their experience, which in the years to follow turned out to be shockingly true and accurate as each participant was to discover. All who were present are now most grateful, since this work remains timeless and true today and beyond.

Lah Rahn Ananda continues channeling to this day in January 2023 now in Earth-Partnership with Master Saint Germain, co-authoring and publishing several Saint Germain books including *The Saint Germain Chronicles Collection*, *Victory For The Soul*, *Rising Above*, *True Compassion For All Humanity in Oneness*, *and other available unpublished works.*

As for you, my Dear Reader, this is your timely opportunity also to choose to become an equally full participant in this and future Masterful work. When you inflow and comprehend these energies, as well as complete the catalytic workbook for your growth, it is Masterfully intended that you be taken and uplifted by your proactive embodiment and practice of this wisdom as a *Friend of Change.*

෧ ෨

Event Begins and
Saint Germain begins to speak

"I AM overjoyed to speak to the hearts of each one of you this day. You are my flag carriers. You are my standard bearers ... standard bearers of the Aquarian Age. As Lord St. Germain I Am indeed overjoyed that each of you would arrange your circumstances this day to be in this presence of the Holy Spirit.

In the Ascended Realm We are, so to speak, clapping our ethereal hands together ... although we have no more hands. As we became un-attached, we gave those up, much in the same way as all of you are becoming unattached to your minds' belief systems of how things should be ...
of how
things should turn out ... and of how you should have your way above all else.
And then giving all that back to Spirit.

In these times upon Planet Earth, change and then more change you shall see, and as I have spoken before, ... change shall become your middle name.

Now, I come to you this day, to nurture your ego consciousness in a way that these parts of you will be able to step aside so that YOU as standard bearers of Spirit, can indeed, walk your walk, dance your dance, find your passion ... rather I need say remember your passion, ... and then each BE in the flow of your dharma's life force.

As always, you have the opportunity for choice – choice of either maintaining the *status quo* with things held in place as best as you can exactly as they are, or of welcoming inevitable change. No risk – so you think.

No burden – your mind may say that. Just get by and cling. Survive and keep things in the status quo. You might even say that the Ego consciousness enjoys being frozen in place ...especially if it feels it is playing a winning game.

And then the Soul-self of you comes forth in a very heartfelt, gracious way as it has, to bring you to this gathering today ... and your H**ighest-self says,** "Yes, I Am in charge. I Am in charge from now on and I Am sorry, my dear Ego, if you are offended. I Am very compassionate. For it is true that I have re-moved your crown and I have placed it upon my head now as the Grand Higher Self and I ask that you as the self ... the small self-centered Ego consciousness vibrating in the lower four bodies of the human being ... I ask now

that you (ego) …now lie down. Thank you very
much for your past contribution
to Me as <u>you (Higher-self)_ wore the crown</u>.

(Higher-self continues<u>) ...</u>
<u>Now it is my turn</u> – I Am choosing to live,
think, converse, act, walk and be One with the
Holy Spirit. And, I will honor you ... I will honor
you my dear Ego as a very important part – as my
ally – as my *surrendered* ally.

**(Saint Germain) You see, when you lie
down in surrender** and when you give yourself
over to Me (your Higher-self), then I have the
benefit of your expertise, your services. You,
Higher-self, are now my loving and surrendered
steward."

So speaks the Soul voice of you, to
manage, console, and court a crest-fallen EGO-
mind. And the voice of the Soul continues:

**"Now it is true in the past you have been able
to have your way.** And just to make you feel
good while <u>I Am</u> transitioning into my light, into
a
vessel that can hold Spirit's light, I will allow you
some of your desires – yes, I certainly will. I will
nurture you, I will hold you as I Am gaining
more and more insight, more wisdom, more

surrender, and more detachment ... I will nurture you. So let's strike a little bargain here ... I will nurture you.

And knowing this, I ask that you, <u>my fine separated Ego consciousness part</u> ... <u>I ask that you become *my friend*</u> – so that, as you say, you get with the band wagon here – climb on board and together we shall make a fine, fine team, you and I. Let us be partners.

Let us be teammates in a fine little connected community of SELF. And I Am grateful beyond expression."

Alright. Now this could well be a conversation that you have with your Ego consciousness on an ongoing basis. For I promise you it will be required every now and then. Even in our more surrendered ones, the ego consciousness will want to stand up and say its say at times. And when this occurs, of course, you have this conversation. You can well see in this scenario how your wishes and desires are apart from your needs. Your beliefs are apart from your knowing, distinct – one from the other.

You can see I Am tendering you so that you yourself can, ironically enough, nurture your ego consciousness with love, and nurture it into surrender. Nurture it with love into its surrender. I can remember in many lifetimes of mine doing this very process and while it is true, some of my lifetimes ... especially in some of the last ... I was in company, consorting, associating, and serving of royalty – kings and queens alike – and I remember oh so well these conversations with my own ego at that time.

Now, I Am going to give you the punch line – I have tendered you long enough!

Today here, *We are tendering the Ego consciousness with Love – We are nurturing your Ego consciousness so that it can die. The separated part of the Ego needs to die. Remember the Shaman? Isn't it ironical that we are nurturing something that needs to die. Well, that's the game. That's the irony!*

When you embrace change, <u>as you are now asked</u>, and you are supported from the Ascended Realms to also embrace all this ... rather, tender it now... the ego consciousness is rather raw.

After all, it has been dethroned – it has been uncrowned. *You are nurturing with love – embracing the ego consciousness so that it can die ... so that you can <u>embrace change</u>. Affix this in your permanent consciousness as the days, weeks, and months ahead bring forth more and more change. Do not worry or fret about what changes are down the road. Let us orchestrate the future. More about this later.*

As was spoken earlier today through this messenger, it is your privilege, it is your Divine power to be in co-creation with ourselves in the present moment without regard to the future or the past... *'in the present moment I do create'. In the past – excluding the present moment – there is no creation future.*

Do you see how that simplifies things for you? And the Ego mind says, yes, but what about all these things in the past? ... think present moment ... present moment.

> **Once in the Moment at present time,
> My Christed self I do align.
> In these moments of reverie,
> Up spring the joys I choose to be.**

The Universe, Spirit, the Creator, however you wish to speak it, is undergoing enormous change. As the Creator evolves so do we evolve all
together – Ascended Spirit, beings on earth, beings in other worlds – evolve together. We're moving – up and up. Evolution has no end.
And so, as change is metered out to each and every one of you individually and through a collective, your choice is: Am I willing to be surrendered to that which the Universe hands me next – and hands me next – and then hands me next? Am I really willing to be surrendered to what the Universe hands me next? Think of it as a large stack of dinner plates where the Universe hands you one plate. You do what you do with it – and then you pick off another one off the stack.

And then it hands you another plate and you do what you do with that – thank you very much. And we hand you another plate, and so on.

And your mind thinks, 'well we're going to get to the bottom of the stack here and when we're at the bottom of the stack we can go back to the *status quo.*

'It's finished and there shall be no more changes!'

Well, it's a little trick that's been played on you. You can count upon change as a constant in Earth Life. Status Quo eventually times out! The plates are sitting on a spring in a well and when you take the last plate off the top up pops another plate, and another plate and another one, ... in a constant streaming flow of life's lessons in *evolution perpetual.*

As Lord Saint Germain of the Seventh Ray and as the Designated Master of the Aquarian Age I ask you, each and every one, to come into partner-ship with me regarding *change* – embracing your Ego so that you can erase separated status-quo desires, and let the changes be all wrapped in love. I know you see that without change we are stuck with the status quo upon Planet Earth.

There's an old saying ... I won't say it exactly as some people say it, but it goes something like; If it isn't broken, don't fix it – just leave things the same as they are. Would you say that supports the status quo?

Well, all of you must know by now that consciousness on the collective and on the individual levels, upon Planet Earth is so very unintegrated and it does need your love and attention in co-operation with ourselves. So as you choose to regard change with love, what's actually happening is that you approach your life in a higher vibration – you actually vibrate at a higher

frequency – *the frequency of love vibrates differently than the frequency of fear.*

Is it not interesting that we always get back to the basics. The human being vibrates in love and the human ...the divining human ... the *divining* human...all humans are divining ... some just don't know it yet, ... the D*ivining human* vibrates in the beginning at the survival level – in the first chakra ... at the base of the spine.

Survival vibration is one of fear. Our process is to work together to raise the consciousness of the divining humanity wherever you may be from the level of human into the level of *human being.* Know well that distinction of human... evolved... to the level of ***human being.*** <u>Beyond The Human Illusion, folks!</u>

So, are we asking of you to be super-human? Indeed we are!! I confess ... being super- human to the point where every circumstance and situation that you encounter is encountered on the level ... the vibratory level, ... of unconditional love. Alright.

Close your eyes for a moment. I Am going to assist you. Close your eyes – if you have anything on your lap take it off your lap and uncross your arms and legs. I Am going to allow Lah Rahn Ananda to stay where he is, although he can arrange himself in a little more optimum pattern.

Visualize in your consciousness change and a fear ... be honest with yourself ... a fear that you have had ... a recent one about a change ... something you're not too sure about and you feel the willies in your stomach ... in the pit of your gut...not too comfortable. Whatever other emotion you might have, bring this up in your consciousness – a fear of change – something you know is up ... and it's not optional. Feel the feeling of it. Feel where it resonates in your body ... the cellular level of fear. Alright, now hold that for a moment ... just hold that right where it is.

Now I want you to open up your brow chakra – your third eye – and out in front of that third eye create a ball of golden white light. Bring it up on your T. V. screen of your third eye – now intensify that light – intensify it more.
So white that it becomes blinding ... it becomes so blinding that you're starting to feel it out in the cells of your body ... your createdness ... *hold the light –*
concentrate – if you don't concentrate then you'll lose it ... hold the light – blinding white – a display of our love – of our vibration in the Ascended Realms.

Now, I want you to go back to where you were and take that fear – center it over your spine – and move it directly upwards up your spine ... up

through the heart chakra ... up through the throat chakra – see the blue ... on up into the brow chakra ... through the indigo ... now take that fear and move it right into the center of the light ... just let it dissipate into the Light.

Notice the feeling you now have in your body ... in the Light... *feel the peace ... feel the relief and the freedom. I ask that you remember this process –a process of giving it back, as you would say, giving fear back to Spirit. And I bless each and every one of you with this gift. It would be wise if you remember it and use it.*

Alright, I think that's about all you can handle for this day. I will be most pleased to answer any questions that you may have before I go.

Participant: Is your last incarnation as the Wonder man of Europe?

St. Germain: That is correct. You see, at that time I was already a member   of the Ascended Realm and it was to be that I come back another time ... one more time ...and that is not to say that I do not come and visit you now ...but I Am speaking of a fully incarnated life-   time ... and to bring light at a particular time when Earth needed Light so very much.

We were in change at that time also ... kings, queens and royalty ... and it had become known that that was no longer working for Me ... and we found another source rather ...   you found *another source through your own evolution.* And

247

then churches came more into popularity as royalty was moved off to the side. Thank you for your question.

Participant: You are welcome.

St. Germain: Thank you, it is my pleasure. Anyone else before I go?

Participant: What is my weakness? My weakest moment?

St. Germain: Your weakest moment ... and this goes for each and every one of you ... your weakest moment <u>is when you choose to be your Ego self, simply put.</u>
The details ... the tentacles that hang down from that, *are your assignments as we hand you different circumstances* ... as you create and draw to the energies of different circumstances – and different aspects of you get honed, initiated, and taught their lessons. Do you see?

Participant: Yes, I'm noticing that during those initiations and those times, there's just a still quiet place that remains even though all other things are happening.

St. Germain: What is that place?

Participant: It is Spirit.

St. Germain: That's right. So you see, you are really two people ... you are two people, and in the process of your evolution you go back and

forth from being one and the other ... now you're Spirit ... now you're back in this lower human vibration ... and now you're Spirit ... and now you're not. And as you evolve there's more of this as Spirit, and less of the lower vibrations. And as you evolve there's more of this and less of this (St. Germain uses Lah Rahn to gesture two opposites) ... and then it all comes to here (gestures the HEART). And now my Beloved Ones, when you reach this point, you are ready to be *taken*. How does that feel? You are ready to be *taken.*

When you shuck this lower part in your consciousness there is a giving and a taking – you all spoke of this earlier today – and when you give up enough of this lower part, then you are ready to be given and to be taken. That is hope ... that is our gift.

Participant: **When you are ready to be taken**, would that mean your Ascension would take you out of your body or would you remain and become a Master of the Planet?

St. Germain: **Thank you, that's a very good question** – it shows that you are looking forward it's where I want you. The answer is it could be both ... it could be one or the other. Many ones that are ready to be taken are left upon this plane to remain into our service. Many are taken to the other side. It depends really upon the Soul agreement that you have with ourselves. It also depends upon your choice at that time ... for you see when you become Divined, you are

One with our consciousness and when you are
One you
know these things. So it's up to your higher self
to commune with ourselves and decide... when an
appropriate time comes along ... when a juncture
is reached.

Participant: There's no way you can tell,
though?

St. Germain: **That would be giving it
away.** You see, I would be shortchanging you to
do your work for you.

In any event, if you are truly **taken**, *others who
are keenly perceptive will observe this miracle
and notice it long before you do.*

If *you announce* to the world your own
Ascension, <u>be assured it is actually your most
untamed and unevolved ego part that is crying out
for the Spiritual self- esteem that it sadly and
pitifully lacks.</u> An Ascended Being asked to
remain now upon Mother Goddess Earth and
serve the Holy Spirit for a period of Earth time,
would simply not make such an announcement
nor be allowed by our Realms to do so.

Humility is a supreme quality unconditionally
required to gain entrance to
the 5th and higher octave Dimensions.

Participant: Thank you, St. Germain.

St. Germain: You are most welcome and you are most loved.

Participant: I'd like to ask one more question in relation to the Soul.

St. Germain: One more.

Participant: **Have there been any physical Ascensions lately or have people left their bodies on the Earth?**

St. Germain: Whether or not a Being leaves the body behind depends upon a number of factors which We Above decide at the time ... it depends in part on the needs of the collective at that time with respect to this being as to how it will serve once the Spirit has Ascended ... how it will serve – or not serve – to leave a body behind. There have been few Ascensions in the last decade. We are optimistic that this number will augment exponentially in the coming 2 decades on Earth, and beyond as well. **Alright, I can't entertain your Egos too much more.**

Participant: **What kind of physical Earth changes** is Mother Goddess Earth going to \]

experience in the next month and what can we do to be there and heal her at that time?

St. Germain: **I will answer your question and before I do, I ask that you look at the first part of that question to see where it comes from?** (Pause)

Alright. Thank you. The physical changes that Mother Goddess Earth will experience are determined in the time and in the moment of the requirement, and the energies then move, stay still, transform, change shape ... *as they need change in the energy of that moment.*

Now with regard to the second part of your question, the healing, "what can I do"? What can we do to do our part to bring forth a healing here of Mother Goddess Earth? **Let me just say your very presence here today is a notable part of that healing. I applaud you all!**

When you go to Mother Goddess Earth in the morning before your day commences and you sit upon her and you do your daily meditation – you are healing Mother Goddess Earth. When you say your decrees heartfully ... as was done in this gathering ... you are healing Mother Goddess Earth.

.

Decreeing need be done by each one of you each and every day ... and remember its possible to do it during your day when the forces of the Ego consciousness come forth and grab you by the throat ... just try and you will be amazed at the results.

Try it once and you may never ever stop. Say a small decree ... you are healing when you say decrees. When you are in prayer, you are healing the planet.

When you bring loving calmness to a situation of chaos, you heal the planet. When you interact with the angelic realms, you are healing the planet – it goes on and on. When you change to love over fear, you're healing the planet. And there are more and more of you – more and more of you gathering in these groups.

You have no idea how the number of groups that I source has increased in just the last couple of years...and we are most grateful,
We are most grateful.

Ascended Spirit cannot do this without you ... *I want you to know that I love you ...* **I Am most appreciative of your keen attention today and the heartfulness that each one of you has brought to your other brothers and sisters and to this gathering. It has been most magnificent and my great pleasure.**

Thank you and good day".

Saint Germain slowly withdraws energy.
from the Vortex.

𝕾𝖆𝖎𝖓𝖙 𝕲𝖊𝖗𝖒𝖆𝖎𝖓

Through Lah Rahn Ananda aka
Gordon Corwin Corwin II
July 26, 1998, Oceanside, California

COLORS OF HAPPINESS

AN

ELEVATED

STATE OF BEING

Behold this magnificent euphoric feeling of Peace and Well-being, a Higher Dimensional state of Joy, Love , and Freedom that flows into and rests within your consciousness, … mind, body, and Soul …. a vibration native to Human DNA, ... with *Free-will to* choose Love and to Be Loved in ONENESS of the All, … while *escalating above* conflicting and negative Earthly influences.

Short of such surrendered ways of Being … while otherwise basking in the status quo harbored by a World of ego–dominated separation … then comes that all familiar fast-track journey along the slippery slope of hope without action, endlessly searching in vain.

Harken to open those doorways that shall appear in your life-stream … opportunities to cross thresholds offering delightful respites of Happiness along your journey, be they flashes or long lived. May an open Heart, Self-Love, purified Self-talk, supportive relationships, and Divine embrace pave your path with Light,

My Dearest Ones.

Saint Germain

Blessings

Saint Germain

Through
Lah Rahn Ananda
02-15-2024

263

COLORS OF
HAPPINESS

SAINT GERMAIN
QUOTES

❧ ❧

"Once in an elevated state of *True Happiness, a magical Divine link is activated.* With this connection thus anchored, a brilliant new mesmerizing journey begins, ushering you into the *original state of Being Fully Human,* freed from burdens of Duality, … at peace in a quizzically joyful silence of harmony and Freedom. Inevitable Earthly influences of many descriptions, negative, positive, societal, and more are Divinely minimized if not fully dissipated, …returned to the Cosmos".

"Entry into this magnificent Domain will require patience and dedication to progress from a *now and again experience* shifting into a *permanent state of True Happines*".

"It may delight you to know that *True Happiness is a companion Blessing,* dwelling beneath the brilliant umbrellas of the 6th and Higher Dimensions of consciousness".

"We Above note this magnificent Soul healing process to occur *simultaneously in tandem* with Ones *Rising Above into Higher Dimensions of consciousness* … from your current Earth World 3rd Dimension into the 5th Dimension of Healing and Transformation, and moving to the 7th Dimension of Unconditional Love … preparatory for entry to the 9th Dimension of absolute purification and Oneness with Source, the All of All".

"**Present Your surrounding elements** of *Love, keen awareness, and an open Heart, ... plus an unfettered willingness to simply Be fully present beyond thought, ... plus other fundamentals that await your discovery,* …then *Happiness* shall embrace the outcome, ... with   delicious deserts emerging, bringing thee the *lasting* Joy, Peace and Freedom you ultimately seek,My Dear Friends.

"*The flash*. Although Happiness may flash, linger, and disappear, … only to unexpectedly reappear, ... take Heart that a ***lasting True Happiness*** is achievable along your journey of Rising Above into Higher Dimensions,

" The *illusion of Happiness* may delightfully alert your senses, sourced by shallow Ego-driven Earthly rewards. The list is long and the illusion is fast fleeting! … Ego rewards, winning, prestige, glory,   sexual gratification of lust, power to dominate, . .. etc. etc. In a flash of time, such enticing and temporary illusions of Happiness rude-

"**Finally, for your insight, consider *True Happiness* an overall energy that blankets underlying tethered elements, including, ...** at minimum::

   An open Loving Heart, where *Happiness* lives

♡ **A carefully tendered *Self-talk* in Divine Alignment**

♡ **A consciousness open to inevitable *change***

♡ ***Trust* in the Universe**

♡ **Willingness to accept *Inner Peace* when it comes**

♡   **Elevating *beyond thinking into BEING* "**!

⊷ ⊶

Blessings

Saint Germain

Through

Lah Rahn Ananda

About the Author

ordon Corwin II, also known as Lah Rahn Ananda, translated literally as 'God Light Messenger', is a native Californian, educated at UC Berkeley, followed by service as a Commissioned US Naval Officer, and by extensive careers in the computer and real estate industries.

In 1995, Gordon clearly heard Lord Saint Germain's resounding and mysterious voice from Above, recruiting him to immediately engage with Ascended Spirit and follow his Soul's calling to reactivate his considerable past life Atlantean DNA channeling abilities, and to begin walking his Dharma to serve Humanity!

As an appointed Masters' Representative, Lah Rahn then began delivering Ascended energies through channeling of the Masters' words and visual media, which would now become his changed and conscious life path. In 1998 he founded The Light of the Soul Foundation, a qualified non-profit entity for advanced Spiritual education and Human philanthropy.

Following years of ego-cleansing by the Masters, Lah Rahn Ji has, for 30 years now, delivered clear and engaging channelings of public and private Spiritual events along with potent and enlightening mentoring of Chelas in The Light of the Soul Vortex in Southern California.

In 2007 he was highly honored to be chosen by Lord Saint Germain to be the Ascended Masters' instrument and Partner to begin, and later complete, this precise and accurate channeling to Earth of The Saint Germain Chronicles Collection, *A Journey Into Practical Spirituality 2008-2014*. In 2020 Lah Rahn again partnered with Saint Germain to write Victory for The Soul, *Relationships that Work, pub 2022, and* RISING ABOVE, *A Journey Into Higher Dimensions, pub 2022, Amazon, Gordon Corwin II,* among other unpublished channelings along with those from Quan Yin and El Morya.

Lah Rahn aka Gordon Corwin currently lives in Oceanside, California and is available for private channelings and group events, as well as public speaking engagements.

Contact:
GordonCorwin24@gmail.com

DISCLAIMER

Light of the Soul Foundation

Established 1998

The Light of the Soul Foundation is a Charitable
non-profit 501 (c) (3) Philanthropic Organization
founded in 1998 by Gordon Corwin, Trustee.
This non-denominational Foundation is dedicated to
The Spiritual Enlightenment of Humanity.
LOSF continues to be harmoniously bonded with
Highland Light Publishers,
sharing this Spiritual mission that includes writing,
publishing, and distributing Masters' books in
addition to delivering live events with wisdom from
The Ascended Masters Above.
"Bringing the Light of Spirit into the _every-day lives_ and
consciousness of the masses
in an increasingly troubled earthly world
… is the practical gift We lovingly offer".

As you now may observe, the collective behavior of Humanity
present dark and pervasive behaviors that prevail without change. Your
kind philanthropy, donations, and bequests provide the financial means
enabling Us to continue serving and delivering _Enlightenment from
Above_, expanding Our outreach of Light.

277

Your donations are transformed into the highest vibrations from Above to all Ones aspiring to reach and live their full Dharma's potential of heightened awareness, Love, Compassion and Soul evolvement ... which awaits Humanity.

Light of the Soul Foundation

Charitable Non-profit 501 (c) (3)

Public Events and Spiritual Counseling

IRS **EIN: 91-1945098**

For Your Gifts, Donations, or Bequest Confirmations, By Check, Credit Card or Wire:

We are deeply grateful to Donors, Contributors and Philanthropists for your fine and generous *Gifts of Grace to uplift The Human Consciousness.*

You are an immensely essential resource that ongoingly empowers Our continuing Outreach.

For two decades, We have delivered gifts of Soul Enlightenment and Practical Spirituality via recently published channeled works, along with public events and   Spiritual readings ... with your generous support!

Many Thanks and Blessings. *You All* **are Most Appreciated!**
Gratefully yours, Gordon Corwin / Lah Rahn
Please Contact: Trustee, Gordon Corwin, Oceanside, CA
92056
Gordoncorwin24@gmail.com

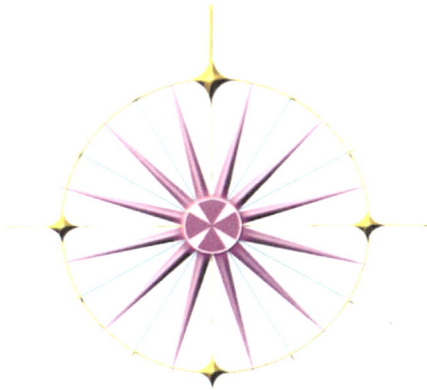

Light of the Soul Foundation
(501)(c)(3)

EIN: 91-1945098

www.ingramcontent.com/pod-product-compliance
Lightning Source LLC
Chambersburg PA
CBRC100735150426
42811CB00065B/1895